R. KRYSTALINE CARBAJAL

Return to Life!

An Empowerment
of the Spirit

KRYSTALINE VISIONS PUBLISHING
Copyright © 2011 R.KRYSTALINE CARBAJAL

All rights reserved under International and Pan-American Copyright Conventions. No part of this book may be reproduced without written permission from the publisher, except in the case of brief quotations embodied in critical articles or reviews; nor may any part of this book be reproduced, stored in a retrieval system, or transmitted in any form or by any means electronic, mechanical, photocopying, recording, or other, without written permission from the publisher.

This book is manufactured in the United States of America.
Cover and text design by R.Krystaline Carbajal
Chapter Illustrations ©Jonathon Earl Bowser www.JonathonArt.com

Published by Krystaline Visions Publishing
Chicago – Flagstaff - Miami - California | TEL 928.613.1082
www.KrystalineVisions.org

Books published by Krystaline Visions Publishing are available at quantity discounts on bulk purchases for premium, educational, fund-raising, and special sales use. For details please call 928.613.1082

Carbajal, R.Krystaline
Return to Life! An empowerment of the Spirit
BISAC: Self-Help/Motivational & Inspirational

ISBN: 0-615-42794-4
ISBN-13: 978-0615427942

WITH LOVE:

For my children Carlitos, Victoria, Robert, Irina, Oscar, and Aruru. Because through you I have experienced the light and love necessary to carry me in the darkness.
Soon, my babies… soon.

For the beacons that have stood as my compass in the storm, and my inspiration in a legacy, Thank you.

To all those people that have touched my life, from childhood until now, from all of you I have learned, and taken the lessons in. Better late, than never!

In memoriam of my elders.
For the many hours of wisdom granted.

Whenever you're lonely and hurting inside, There will always be someone right by your side.

Whenever you think your faith is used up, That someone will come and raise it back up.

Don't you ever forget how to pray, It doesn't matter what people say.

'Cause people only think their smart, But true feelings come from the heart.

-R.KRYSTALINE CARBAJAL

Guardian Angel, *a poem*

5.28. 93

R.Krystaline Carbajal

CONTENTS

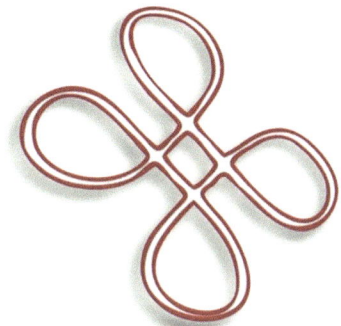

AUTHOR'S NOTE viii
OPENING YOUR PERCEPTION 11
BECOMING AWARE 25
SUBMITTING 43
ACCEPTING THE PAST 53
RULES OF THE GAME: 61
THE CALM: 77
MONEY, HEALTH and LOVE 87
BALANCE & CHANGE 93
THE PURPOSE OF PRAYER 113
MEDITATIONS: 125
ABOUT THE AUTHOR: 129

R.Krystaline Carbajal

AUTHOR'S NOTE

I commend you for having the courage to admit that these humble writings might in some way help you. Oftentimes, when we are so wrapped up in the happenings of life, we tend to forget the little things, including the small voices, or reason we hear in our head, that tell us when something doesn't feel right. When things do feel right, we may ignore these feelings or neglect to appreciate them. We just don't pause.

I want you to understand that you will find no power in this book, and these words hold no special meaning. It is only within yourself that you will find what you seek. It has always been there—you just turned down the volume so that you couldn't hear it or feel it—but it is there. The power to set yourself free is within you, and I cannot tell you where. Only you can know that. Through this journey we are about to embark on, we will set sail to many ideas and exercises that will help you find the hidden code and unlock the mysteries you hold within yourself.

Today, you take the first step to complete freedom. The freedom you once knew, only as a child. This freedom is free from worries, pain, suffering, hate, and lovelessness, all of which poison your mind and spirit, lower your vibrational field, tie you

Return to Life! An empowerment of the Spirit

down to their reality, and make you their prisoner. You have become a prisoner of your own reality, and as the statement implies, you put yourself there.

We will go through several doors. These doors can be opened only if you have taken from the book, and found the hidden code within yourself to unlock them. Beyond each door, you will only find the best within. Discover all the things, you will come to learn, that have been unconsciously or automatically recorded and absorbed by yourself, and await you. The hidden ambitions of your spirit, the karma that belongs to only you, the freedom, and the love you seek... and all of this, you will give to yourself. No one else can pretend to hold the key, because you are the key.

As you pass through each door, you will feel these effects immediately. Your life will begin to change. Change is good, it is nature's way. With each door that opens, you will feel closer and closer to your goal, until eventually you pass through the last door, and you Return to Life!

Light and Love always,

OPENING YOUR PERCEPTION

In order to go through life, we are given certain attributes. These attributes are bestowed to us at birth: mind, body, spirit, intuition, and perception. None of us is perfect, in fact, it is human nature, to be imperfect, and some people would argue that it is this imperfection that prevents us from ever setting ourselves free. It is quite the opposite. The first step in unlocking the first door to create change is opening your perceptions.

As a given right we have minds and bodies, with which we function every day. What of the spirit, intuition, and perception? These are often neglected, mainly because people ignore what they can't see or touch. Can you see your body? Yes. Can you touch your body? Yes. Do you accept that your body is there? Yes. Great! You have passed the test of acceptability for the body, and we all recognize and acknowledge that it is there.

What of the mind? Let's go through the same test of acceptability. Can you see your mind? No. Can you touch your mind? No. Do you accept that your mind is there? Yes. Oops! What is wrong with this picture? How can you answer "*No*" to two out of three and still accept that something is there? Are we imagining things? Is the mind pure fantasy or wishful thinking, or is it that we *choose* to alter our perception to an open one, in order to accept the existence of the mind?

Some will argue that our mind is in our brain, and the human brain *is* something you can see and touch. However, what *is* our brain but water, electricity, sugar, and cells? Our mind is our conscious self, our thoughts, and our intelligence. Can we see or touch our thoughts or our intelligence? Because we do not see these, do we believe that they do not exist? These questions, are questions that are often answered with a firm *no*.

Does our mind tell us that it exists? Is our mind something separate from our consciousness? Why does it seem like our mind knows more than we do? I mentioned that the hidden key to unlocking all the doors to freedom is held within you. Why do we not know this already? Is it possible that our mind is separate from our personality? If this is so, who am I really?

The answers to all of these questions are inside you. You already know the answers; you may just *choose* not to hear them. For example, you may have witnessed an event and walked away with a certain *perception* of the events that you tell others about. As time goes on, someone who witnessed the same event recalls the details differently than you, and suddenly you remember an added detail, and then another, until you realize that you have an altered perception. You blocked out details that indeed were there. You did not forget them, because you remembered them, as if they were stored in your memory for later retrieval. You play back the memory and realize that there are certainly things you left out before. How can this happen?, and why do some people not experience the lapse in details?

This experience is the same for people who witness a crime or an accident. Some are very "good witnesses," as some would say, and others cannot remember what color the cars in the accident were, which way the assailant ran, or what the thief was wearing. Why are memories for some people like 'misty water colored memories', as the song says, and others give vivid accounts with full details? The answer lays in *perception.*

A person with *open* perception is willing to take in all the information that is fed to them. This means using the five senses (touch, smell, sight, hearing, and taste) as well as mind, sprit, and intuition. To open your perception means to be receptive to all things that come to you and to what surrounds you at every second of every day.

Most people take the five senses for granted. For instance, some have closed themselves off to an important form of perception, sight. For blind people, sight in its full capacity is not gone. It is scientifically proven than in blind persons their sensitivity to other senses is heightened. The idea that blind persons have lost their sight, or vision, is not completely correct. They cannot experience color or light in the same way that others can, but they "see" things in ways that most others cannot due to their opened perception. People who are blind do not have the barrier of being fooled by what is physically in front of them. They rely on *all* their senses— including mind, spirit, and intuition—allowing themselves to "feel" life.

Perception is a powerful thing and not to be taken lightly. Some people already know this. Perception can free you from your self-inflicted prison or put you in a merry prison of your own. Perception can be turned against you, and you should realize it is the most important key of all. Opening your perception, does not mean you are to fall victim to anything, or anyone. Opening your perception is meant to give you the ability to make up your own mind about what to do next, and to follow your true path. It does not mean falling victim to others that have learned to manipulate perception or becoming manipulative yourself.

The "good manipulators of perception" are people who have dedicated themselves to helping others achieve the same openness that they have experienced. Once you experience open perception, you obtain a feeling of true satisfaction, a feeling that leaves behind doubt, fear, uncertainty, and worry.

Once you open your perception, you begin to understand the principles on which life as a whole is built. You will "see" the world in a different light, and the first step is to stop asking "Why?" To open your perception, you must understand this concept. You must stop questioning. You must accept. You must let go. You must give up. You must release control. You must gather the strength within and say "I submit." When a belief structure is in shambles, it is sometimes wiser to demolish it, start from scratch, and build a better model.

When someone is drowning, he panics, and the more he panics, the faster he sinks. It is not until you relax, release, and let go that you may perhaps survive the drowning incident, and finally float and go where the flow takes you. Life is like the ocean. You must release and go wherever it takes you. But it is not until you relinquish control, that you will experience this peace.

It is curious to hear people say that life does not favor them because things do not go their way. This is a perception. The more this person thinks this way, the more this thought will manifest itself. Although this person believes that things are out of control, it is them in fact out of control. We have the power within to shape our surroundings. And here goes a statement that will seem contradictory: *It is not until you release control that you will enable your perceptions to control your surroundings.*

EXERCISE TO OPEN YOUR PERCEPTION

I recommend that you try this exercise with more than one person; it can be friends, your children, your significant other, or anyone you choose, until you can comfortably do it alone. Read through this exercise first, become familiar with it, and then visualize it in your mind, as you do it. If you are in a group, perhaps someone can read the instructions out loud.

1)   Remove all distractions. Many people like to play music to induce meditation or concentration, but the purpose of this exercise is not to be distracted or "influenced" by the sounds of music—rather become in tune with the sounds of life around you.

2)   Sit or lay down, whichever is most comfortable. Close your eyes, and just breathe out deeply. Relax your arms, relax your fingers, relax your neck, and shoulders. Breathe out deeply.

3)   Now relax your legs, and relax your ankles and feet. Keep your back straight; do not slouch. Tilt your head back. Breathe out deeply. Concentrate on the sounds of the life stirring within you. Picture your heart pumping blood through your body. Picture your blood running through your veins. Hear the beautiful rhythm played by the

pumping of your heart. Hear your heart beat. Feel the energy of your being surge within you. Call on it to recharge you.

4) Now step out of yourself and listen. Listen to the sounds of life outside of you. Feel the energies that surround you. Can you perceive the location of your fellow neighbor? Whether it is a person sitting next to you, an animal or pet. If alone, you can even tune into your neighbors next door, or persons near you. Without sight, can you feel and hear the rhythm their body plays, just as your own.

5) Slowly come back now. Bring your energy close. Breathe deeply. Relax, release, and let go. Do not fear. Do not question the feelings you just experienced. Breathe deeply. Open your eyes now. How do you feel?.

If you performed this exercise alone, take some time to write down your experience in a notebook, or a journal. If you were in a group discuss your feelings and your experiences.

Return to Life! An empowerment of the Spirit

Describe your experience: _____

_____

_____

_____

_____

_____

_____

You've taken the first step toward opening your perception.

I will give you an example from my own life. I experienced a reluctance and fear to open to my perceptions, and I refused to become aware, as human nature most of the time entraps us. I was ignorant. This story starts with a bright young woman that people said was destined for great things. I saw life with the vigor and sense of wonderment that only a child sees. I was trained as an oil painter, at the tender age of nine, by a famous painter in Mexico, and

I became her studio assistant in exchange for lessons. During my apprenticeship, I learned the beautiful life of colors and expression. This experience changed me, it taught me that color was all around us, and the privilege of placing them on a canvas, paper, or another medium was a gift bestowed on me and all artists alike. It made me understand that my perception of color before this experience was jaded and incomplete.

I was also introduced to music at the age of five. I started piano lessons and was given lessons in theory; I practiced at home on a small electric organ my dad got me. In grammar school, I was introduced to an instrument that no one wanted to play because it was cumbersome and required a higher level of love for the craft of music: the trombone. I took the challenge from my band director and applied myself like no other. I soon became so enthralled with the instrument that my skills quickly grew, that a raised to a level that no one thought possible, especially not in the short time of one year. Musicians that practiced and played this instrument longer did not advance this fast. Then something wonderful happened: I was asked to audition for the Chicago All City High School Band, for third chair in the band. This band was composed of only the best players from the best high schools citywide. But wait... I was only in sixth grade! 'No matter', I was told, 'just show up to the audition.'

Early on a Saturday morning, I showed up to the practice space, and as I entered, I heard the sweetest melodies floating through the air. I could literally close my eyes and be transported to a place of peace and wonderment. With my heart racing and eyes wide open, I continued to the designated location set for my audition. As I walked into the room, I heard musical scales being played with such precision and speed. I saw others auditioning and playing their instruments with such confidence and vigor that it made me feel simple and small. It effectively deflated any sense of confidence that I might have walked in with. I gripped my case, prepared for my turn, and prayed that I would not make a fool of myself.

When it was my turn, I saw my grammar school band director gather with the lead band director and the audition director. They convened and whispered, occasionally turning back to look at me. I felt my heart racing as they signaled for me to come in to the audition room. A tall, poised director said, "So you are the special case everyone is talking about." How do you respond? Fear set in for lack of confidence that I be, at any level, anywhere near as good as the musicians before me. While I was frozen in this almost surreal experience, this director placed his hand on my shoulder and said, "Relax, and just play from the heart. Forget that we are here and just play."

I had prepared to play a choral piece by Bach and had practiced countless hours, and yet at this moment I felt paralyzed. I was asked to do some scales to warm up, and as I picked up my instrument and I began to play, I forgot that anyone was in the room. I became engaged in the arrangement that I was playing, and I gave the notes all the love I had within. I was engulfed in the notes, and the room became filled with the enchanting melody. At the end of the piece, there was a silence, as the final note remained in the air. As it slowly died out, I opened my eyes to find the director with his eyes closed too. With his applause, at that moment I felt "aware."

Regardless of my age and grade, a huge exception was made, and I was accepted into the All City High School Band, while only in 6th grade. With the band, I played my heart out, each time diving deeper and deeper into the music, and as I submitted to it, it seemed an experience that transcended time and space. I was surrounded by beautiful sounds that, when I closed my eyes, became dancing colors in my mind. I was privileged to perform at Chicago's prestigious Orchestra Hall, home of the Chicago Symphony Orchestra, which was the culmination of my childhood dream in music.

I had allowed my perception to be opened, and I gave in to the will of the path I chose. Only then did I feel this "connection" with everything, and I saw the world in a different light. To quote one of my favorite thinkers, Ralph Waldo Emerson, "Do not go where the path may *lead*, instead go where there is no path and leave a *trail*."

I was free.

BECOMING AWARE

Be sure that you have completed the exercise to 'Open Your Perception' in the previous chapter. You must experience the feeling of freedom that the exercise gives you in order to move on to becoming aware.

Opening your perception for the first time might leave you with a feeling of accomplishment. Some say it makes them light-headed, because the experience is so intense. In either case, once you open your eyes and complete the exercise, you will never see life in the same way again.

Once you open your perception, it is like awakening from a dream. The process is not immediate, but the results are. The path to becoming aware is through opening your perception, seeing things for what they are. All of this, I want you to know does not require any change in your beliefs. In fact, it will enable anyone to follow the path they have chosen with stronger vigor and awareness of the path.

Becoming aware is the final step in opening your perception. Those who become aware truly enable themselves to will, and they become in control of their intentions, path, destiny, karma, and life. As the saying goes, "Ignorance is bliss." We often yearn for illusion, for counterfeit pleasures.

Forget about being someone really important, being famous and rich in a world of complete illusion. The counterfeit version is an easy ride. Real meaning and virtue take a lot of effort.

Have you ever felt that something was destined to happen? Do you think you're in full control? There are no coincidences, no random events, and no casual happenings. Every event of your life is exactly what you made it to be—part of your personalized program to complete your life's mission.

The tapestry of world history is unrolling, all according to a plan, yet you have complete freedom to choose how to react. There are events that will happen. History has a path.

Your life has a path, and it's up to you to decide if you will embrace it, and make it happen according to your will. If you seize the moment, you will find that unique role waiting for you. Ancient tradition teaches that the entire world was created *for you*. The entire world was created *in you*.

The entire world is a stage, and you are in the starring role... It's real. Here you are in your own custom-designed world. It is filled with everything you need to bring yourself to perfection, and that will in turn pull the entire universe into alignment. There will be a lot of situations to push you to the limit and bring out the full spectrum of your very own subtle qualities.

There is a difference between knowing the path and walking the path. The hundreds of thousands of moments allotted to you on this planet are precious. At the moment of birth, you were given the gift of forgetfulness so you could learn anew with interest and wonder. You had to learn to walk, to speak, to think, and to question. Now you stand poised at the edge, awake at last, asking the right questions, driven by the very core of your soul.

Remember: there are no coincidences. Everything happens for a reason. Everything happens as a direct reaction to any given action, by either yourself or another. Tap into your path, strength, perception, and awareness, and you will make things happen.

After reading all of the above, many people become afraid. The fear comes from the human panic factor we discussed before. People fear what they do not understand and stay within their own comfort levels. It is the same reason why long lost love in couples is ignored for the creature comforts of being used to someone.

Becoming accustomed is the most human of all instincts, but it is also the most damaging. Human pre-dispositional behavior is a funny thing for the same reason. Think of people who live by the edge of an active volcano; after the volcano causes a disaster, people flee but then come right back. They rebuild and resettle until the next disaster. Why? Because the people are used to being there. They have reached a comfort level. They are afraid of what might happen if they move to a strange place, after generations of tradition. They have not opened their perception and become aware. They have not experienced what life has to offer. They are simply letting themselves be influenced by the reactions of the actions of others.

Becoming aware is power. All great leaders have embarked on the path of opening their perceptions. They see things others do not. This is why they lead, because they are trying to show others the vision, the path of opening your perception.

Every time you are at a lecture, seminar, or class, you are attempting to open your perception. Every time something happens to you, the reason why the question "Why?" does not make sense, is because life is trying to open your perception. If you think about it, we go about life with blinders on, that prevent us from seeing the signs. The subtle changes, incidents, and sometimes in our mind 'coincidences', they all point us towards our destination—or path. We ignore them or mock them. So it is indeed not life's fault that bad things happen, but only our own.

Just by reading this chapter and performing the exercise in the previous chapter, you embark on the road to becoming aware. This will not happen overnight—neither will it take years, unless you choose to remain with the blinders on. Stop saying *'no', 'I can't',* and *'why?';* Just live, experience, feel, see, enjoy, share, help, give, teach, love, and heal.

By becoming aware, you will transcend boundaries that once seemed impossible to cross. In order to become aware, you must open your perceptions, and accept all as it comes to you, push back on the wave of what seems life's set of distractions, and shape your future by bending it to your own will. '*All*' means the good and the bad, as without one there would not be the other.

To quote Deepak Chopra, "You are not in the world, the world is in you." Stop waiting for opportunities; If there are none, make them. You *are* the creator of your own destiny, your own path, and your own consequences. People often misinterpret the wise saying, "Ride the wave," as they think it means to let life float past them, to lose a sense of their surroundings, to tune out. No wonder these people cannot find the peace they seek, as the statement means the complete opposite.

Riding the wave implies that we have to let go of the control we so desperately seek in our lives. It means that we give up constantly making, or seeking, obstacles and excuses; instead choose to see opportunities and make choices. We choose to *tune in* instead of becoming numb, and by doing this, we reconnect with our surroundings. We experience that sunset in the city just as we do in the open country. We stop and appreciate the people around us. We pay attention to the details that we often once ignored. Smells and sounds become alive; colors gain a vivid impact. This is when you truly begin to *see*.

When we make excuses and reasons, we isolate or limit ourselves—we hold ourselves back. The true beauty of experiencing life this way—in a manner in which everything seems new—is that it is beautiful. When you choose to see the world in this non-judgmental way, every time you look you will discover something new.

Becoming aware means being able to see beyond the immediate future and take a leap of faith in ourselves. We should be able to trust in ourselves unconditionally and take the leap of faith with our eyes closed. Perhaps you did at one time, but not anymore. That is the faith you seek. Becoming aware means that you must trust yourself. Have faith that all the answers that you seek are inside you, even if you don't see them right away. Trust that in time, as we need to know, the answers you seek will come. Becoming aware shows that you understand this commitment. Accept that you understand that everything cannot be as you wish at all times, but that everything can always be as it should be.

It seems like a contradictory statement, but if you think about it, it is not. The main reason for our disappointment, stress, or anxiety comes from the fact that we want things our way, *now and always*. There is a funny fact about this self-made, waiting-to-get-you, sure-to-fail-every-time plan. We understand that we cannot always have our way, and yet, when we do not achieve something, we feel these emotions.

Do you see the malfunction in this plan? We set ourselves up for failure willfully.

Why not aspire for success as it comes? Why not be inspired to seek success, yet accept and appreciate failure for the lessons learned from it? We can choose to not be upset when we did not obtain what our capricious little heart wanted. This is the heart of the saying, "Lo Qué Será, Será." What will be, will be. This leap of faith means that we accept that it is impossible to always have our way. When we do, we should appreciate it as much as when we do not.

When we can learn to see the lessons of our failures, we can accept that things happen as they should, regardless of how we feel about it.

The key to becoming aware and riding the wave is to understand the serendipity in these situations and statements.

Know that you hold a purpose even if you are not exactly sure of what that is.

Understand that you hold the power to shape your own reality by opening your perception. Believe in yourself, and have faith that the answers you seek are within.

Give yourself credit, take a deep breath, buckle up, and enjoy the ride!

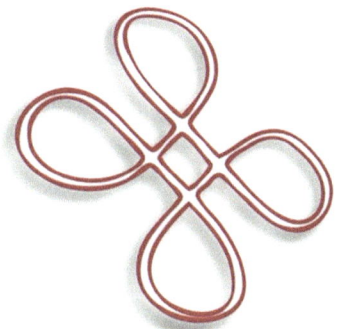

LIFE LESSONS

A lot of the experiences and anecdotes I share here are from my own life. I have chosen to share my journey and some of the darkest moments of my life, as I am the perfect example of how one *can* return to life, even after giving up all hope. All that you have read so far does not have to match your own experience exactly; if you did not take painting or music lessons, you can experience the same awe or sense of open perception.

These moments I share with you are examples of how simple it is to submit and let go, and once you do that, you can finally take control and experience all of life's wonders. Everyone has something different for them in their passions, or path—just follow it. Do not fear, as I did in the story I am about to share, the ability to survive. Change is within us all, and the things that happen to us as a result of our own choices do not mean that you cannot wake up and take command once you become aware again.

As you read about my choices, I hope you will see parallels in your own choices. Remember that as human beings we possess free will and we are free to enforce it. However, it is doing so with an open perception and becoming aware that changes us, our environment, and our actions. The reactions that follow can only hold the riches you seek, which is to be spiritually awakened and to take charge.

ANOTHER PIECE OF MY STORY:
The tragedy of living with blinders on

At fifteen, it seemed that I "had it all," and I was at the height of what I thought would be my life path. I was introduced to a suitor. Enchanted with musical talents and mutual intelligence, we spent hours talking about music, art, life, philosophy. I married this person at a very young age (my mid-teens) and embarked on a treacherous road that changed my life forever.

It all began simply enough: I had my first child at the age of eighteen. I was filled with joy and felt I was the luckiest and most blessed girl in the world. Blessings soon turned into feelings of regret. With my growing responsibilities as a new mother, I ceased to play music, and I left other things I loved behind. Painting still graced my life, and through this medium, I had some freedom of expression even though I felt that I was losing control of my life. My new life in this relationship left me feeling a sense of emptiness, as I felt I had become a "trophy" to be owned and displayed with pride.

I fell out of touch with my friends and family, as I was told that my priorities should be my "new" family. I was told to apply myself to our new business and to forget the childish practices. As I had more and more placed on my plate, including the birth of my daughter at nineteen, I felt more and more boxed in. It was then, at a very bad moment I lost contact with more family members, including my mother and father.

At home, I was constantly put down emotionally and scolded for anything less than perfection. I had graduated at the top of my class, attended a math and science academy, and received a business management degree before my mid- twenties. My performance as a woman, mother, and businesswoman, however, was never enough.

It is true, what they say, that some people perform better under pressure, and I took the mounting insults and put-downs as part of achieving greatness. As the years went by, our business became very successful and lucrative. For most people, making so much money at such a young age would bring a sense of achievement, and yet something was missing.

Although I was happy at work and did feel a sense of accomplishment, I was always sad. At home, I was continually abused emotionally but kept a "blind eye" to it. At home, I was "walking on eggshells" all the time. I learned to avoid words or situations that would upset my counterpart. As drugs and alcohol came into the mix, things got worse. I was slapped and shoved for poor performance at work, and warned to "produce more." The only pure light in my life was the love of my children.

What had happened to the bright, free young woman who once lived life with such fervor? What was I supposed to do next? Were money and success all there was to life? Was buying a new car and clothes the culmination of my journey?

Was I condemned to live this life of sadness and

alienation in exchange for material goods? Was I to sacrifice the happiness of my children? My children were my only solace and joy, and for them, I was willing to pay a steep price.

After more than seven years of physical, verbal, and emotional assaults (always followed by flowers, favors, jewelry, and promises to never repeat the abuse), I decided that this was the life I was meant to live. The consequences I suffered bought my children's safety. I had suffered many broken noses, a dislocated jaw, and numerous other bumps and bruises.

The culmination of the domestic violence was an argument, turned into a fight, which ended in my being lifted about two feet off the ground, as I was being strangled. This event would leave me paralyzed and forever changed. At one point I even thought it would be my undoing, but it turns out, surviving this attack was my strength, as it gave me courage and purpose. Living, experiencing, and overcoming were now the best parts of my life, and so began my journey into life.

The tale of how I became paralyzed and overcame it, is a tale on its own entirely, one I will share one day in another book. However, because the complete sense of my emotional state is needed here, in order to understand the feelings I wish to describe, I will share a portion of this tale. The events seemed to be just a bad dream as I lost consciousness, and everything went black...

On a hot, sticky day in New Orleans (before Hurricane Katrina), I woke up and looked around. I was in total shock when I saw that I was in a room that seemed to come straight out of the 1940s. There were many beds in the room, separated only by mobile dividers. As I panned the room from my line of sight, I realized that a doctor was standing at the edge of my bed, looking like he was trying to make sense of a puzzle, as he stared at my medical chart.

As I engaged in a conversation with him, I remembered my attacker's words, "Stick to the story." This meant that should I choose to say the truth of the events, my consequences would be worse. In my mind, telling the truth would end up my attacker in jail, but leave me stranded with no one to reach out to, and no way to take care of my children while paralyzed. What to do?

 I chose to lie. I chose to say "I tripped over some luggage in my hotel room, and hit the back of my head on the table", this was the story I was drilled to tell. The doctor wasn't buying what I was selling. He told me that the ligature marks on my neck suggested that I had been strangled, and the gripping force had almost severed my spinal cord.

The result was a badly bruised spinal cord with a contusion (swelling). He said they were injecting steroids to reduce the swelling but that there was no guarantee that it would work. From now on healing was up to my body. It was not likely that I would walk again. What a shock it was to hear that! At that moment, it was hard to comprehend the meaning behind his words; they seemed to float past me as I was lost inside my own thoughts and speculations about my future.

His voice seemed to dim out become almost an echo, far away. It was only then that I realized that I was not able to move anything from the neck down. I had ignored the feeling, or rather lack thereof, while entranced by listening to the doctor.

How would I survive now? How would I care for my children? If I healed, would this happen again? Will I heal? Where did I go wrong with my life? As the doctor walked away, I closed my eyes, and let out a big sigh. *Why me?*

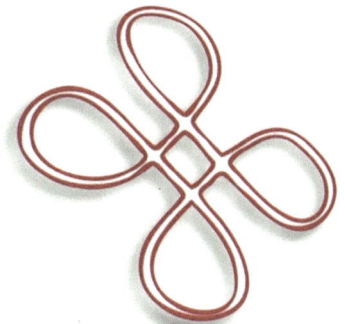

SUBMITTING

After reading the tragedy that befalls those who live with blinders on, as I did, it seems to contradict all reason. The escalating violence in my life set the stage for a future sequence of events. As it was happening, I was so wrapped up in the fear of losing financial status and public "face" that I lost sight of my path and my goals.

I had to hit rock-bottom first to become aware that I needed to leave the madness behind, remove my shackles, and move forward in life.

There are some spiritual beliefs that state that all paths lead to our destiny. I was at a crossroads, a fork in the road, a pivotal point. I needed to accept, and make a choice to submit. To stop asking 'why?' and to stop living with so much regret; To stop blaming and start accepting; To stop fighting the reasons and just relax to follow the flow, wherever it will take you—as I did, you must do—and just "Submit."

I had to come to terms with the fact that I may not walk again. I had to depend on nurses and, worst of all, my abuser to feed me and care for me. I spent my birthday in a hospital bed, surrounded by others trapped in their own consequences as a result of their choices. Laying there in despair, disappointed that I had failed myself, I opened my eyes and saw a priest. He was tall and calm, and he came to me with such faith and goodwill in his face that I did not feel threatened. He asked if I was religious. I told him that I believed everything happened for a reason, although I knew not what it meant for me now. I was at the point of acceptance.

He asked me if I would pray with him, and as I did, and he placed his hand on my arm (which I saw but did not feel), I felt myself enter into a deep, relaxing sleep.

I saw an abyss of white everywhere I looked. I saw my recently deceased grandfather, who had always been my pillar of encouragement in my life. I walked to him, and he held me and smiled. This hug seemed to last forever, and

Return to Life! An empowerment of the Spirit

I was enveloped by a love that, until then, I had only felt from holding my children--A love and a light that was so unconditional that it filled my very being.

After this experience, I realized that I had been looking at life all wrong. I saw a glass half-empty instead of half-full. I had not realized how lucky I was to even be alive. The fact that there was a remote possibility, no matter how minute, that I could regain movement was better than no chance at all. The look on that priest's face as he approached me to offer solace was an epiphany; I was left breathless by the moments of light and love I experienced when I closed my eyes, and the memory of that moment transports me there instantly. Everything was not as bad as I thought.

As the days, months, and years passed, I slowly progressed from moving a finger to upper body motion. Eventually, I regained my leg movement and am now walking again. Although this experience has left me forever changed with a life of physical and emotional pain I must deal with on a day to day basis, I cannot help to stop and think: Was this experience to teach me that we do not see the gifts we have been given, such as life itself, until they are taken away?

The truth is... that I am alive, and that alone should be enough. This experience changed me and impacted my life in a way so profound that I felt compelled to recover, to return to the path I once walked, and to complete my life's goals. Although many painful months followed, and strenuous physical therapy took place, once I returned home, I was determined to allow myself to heal, not just physically, but emotionally and spiritually—to become whole again.

The physical pain that came with my recovery was unimaginable, but no matter what happened, I moved forward. I was facing a lifetime filled with constant pain. I received injections in my spine every three months and trigger-point injections in my back every three weeks to keep the muscles from going into spasm. I tried acupuncture and any other holistic and experimental treatment available.

Almost two years later, all the struggle paid off, when I succeeded in beating the odds. I never gave up hope that the effort would be worth it. I had faith in myself. My plan was to take charge and make my destiny work for me. At one time, "submitting" seemed like a bad idea, but eventually I learned that it was the best decision of my life.

Make no mistake I was not giving up, I submitted to the fact that I was disabled and that I move forward instead of being stuck in the moment. I submitted to the fact that I could not control the speed of my recovery or my recovery itself directly. I gave up the mentality that other people's opinions mattered more than my own. I remembered why I had given up the activities that made me feel free and alive. As I opened up my perception and realized how much I had missed, I felt as though a veil had been lifted and saw life in a different light.

I reflected on the experiences of my past and began to chart my future. It was all so surreal the way that the weight was lifted off my shoulders. I was raised all my life to be an overachiever, and failing or losing were not good options. To say to a person like that "You have to give up control in order to gain it" sounds like a bunch of mumbo jumbo. When I first thought of it, I had to check myself a few times to make sure I hadn't lost any screws. It made sense in my head, but logically it didn't make any sense at all.

The meaning of this statement was made clear to me in the journey described in this chapter. For you, it might be another situation, set of situations, or moments. In my workshops and seminars I hear stories from people that leave me feeling even luckier than ever. I feel inspired by other's courage and determination, and others have said the same of me. In the end, our lives are all up to us; they are what we make them to be. It is our own interpretation that matters: That is the ultimate truth.

Submitting is the act of lowering your barriers and welcoming trust and wisdom into your circle. It is the perception of new moments now being seen in full light. It is giving into the fact that in controlling nothing we control it all, another seemingly contradictory sentence, and this gives way to the inner peace we desire.

We constantly run around in the rat race we call life, in a hurry like the White Rabbit in *Alice in Wonderland*, crying, "I'm late! I'm late! I'm late!" Did you ever figure out what you where late for?

We never know how far we dig ourselves in until it is almost too late, but therein lays the key to this riddle. Almost too late is better than never. For those of us whose life events seem to have passed all reasonable deadlines for repair, it is never too late.

Knowing that your intentions line up with your heart's

desires and your actions gives you the courage and determination to see these ideas through. You create a reality of your own design and fulfill your wishes. Suddenly 'Lo Qué Será, Será' carries a whole new meaning, and things begin to make more sense.

Try these actions in your own life. Change your perception and become aware. Submit to your destiny, and follow the path of your own choosing, the one that lights your fire. Find the passion that flows through your veins. If you are seeking it out still, challenge yourself with as many experiences as possible. Volunteer, work as an intern, or dedicate yourself to a cause. These are good ways to observe others that are good at what they do and experience other people's passions.

Use your time to search inward. Look back. They say that hindsight is twenty-twenty: as we look back, we see things that we missed before.

There are always moments in your life that point to who you will be and the path you will follow. People often do not look back until they have some of their goals, but what if we were to use that same process to find our roadmap to the future? For example, as a child I gathered my cousins, young and older, and had them sit down and listen as I taught them something. They used to call me "teacher dolly."

Today, in my workshops and seminars, I am still getting people to sit down so that I can teach them something.

At heart, we have always known what we want from life from a very young age. We will say "I want to be an astronaut" or "I want to be the president." We can even visualize ourselves in the role. That is the beauty of childhood—we are not hindered by an overwhelming amount of choices or stimulation.

Our imagination can run wild, and we can dream. It was this way for me. So when do we lose this? the ability to see one's goals in our mind's eye. As a curiosity, whenever I speak to people I ask about their goals and dreams.

It has been my experience that about 80 percent of the people I spoke with, agree they remember loosing this. But then a curious thing came out of these statistics, I noticed that more than half, of the same people I talked to, needed to be taken back to their childhood and asked very specific questions in order to recall.

This curious behavior comes from locking our desires so far away, under lock and key in our psyche, that we make ourselves forget. We are prisoners of our own making. We hold ourselves back from our full potential. We limit our ambitions to those that we feel are *safe* or *realistic*, but what is safe? What is realistic?

Isn't it all a matter of how you perceive it?

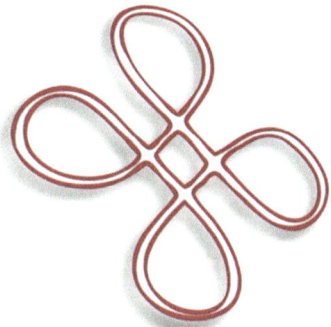

ACCEPTING THE PAST

Although many traumatic, painful, and unspeakable things have happened in my past, I chose to take the open perception that as these events surrounded me, and perhaps defined my present, nothing would define my future but my own decisions.

I chose instead to grasp the smiles, the love, the tears of joy, and the victories I sought to understand. What we *do* carries consequences, and the choices we make take us to where we need to be. I have left all that pain and a life of abuse behind me, and I have made it my choice to push forward and find comfort in accepting my past.

In the beginning, I could not talk about my physical abuse without reliving it. I would mentally be transported to that time and place, and, with every word, I felt the pain all over again. It is easier to suppress, ignore, and avoid what they call an "open wound," but if I have learned one thing in my years of survival it is that talking about it helps tremendously.

I found a certain peace being in a room with others who have been through similar woes. It doesn't matter if it is Alcoholics Anonymous, Narcotics Anonymous, a group of domestic violence or cancer survivors, or pain management focus groups—it helps!

Knowing that another individual has experienced a similar situation makes you feel all the more human. It brings a reality filled with light at the end of the tunnel. Just attending an event or meeting is a victory, considering that it takes many people all their lives to build up the courage to go and they still might not participate. Why? Ignorance, shame, embarrassment, fear—pick one. They are all misconceptions and prisons built of our own accord.

It took me a year and a whole lot of running and hiding to build up the confidence to attend a meeting for domestic violence victims. When I finally did, it was something like trying to treat an illness yourself; once you see a doctor and learn about your options for healing, you feel much better. This is a prime example of the statement, "We have nothing to fear but fear itself." We build our own walls and obstacles without realizing it, like a knee jerk reaction.

I was afraid of having to recount my story, to strangers no less, but as I listened to the others in the group, even as you choose to keep your silence, I realized that it was okay to not be perfect. Why was I so ashamed? Who am I afraid to disappoint? The questions terrified me, but as I began facing them, the ice began to melt around me, and I started to see my core.

The first time you speak up is always hard. It is like a farewell, knowing that this is the last time this story will have a hold on you. Telling the story will hurt less and less, as you share and listen. This is in essence, the core of the human condition: The act of caring. The people in the room with you are there because they care. As you allow yourself to lift the blinds from your vision and absorb these moments, you feel the humanity in the room with you. You feel what it is like to breathe and be alive. To allow others to touch your life through their experiences is to connect and to live.

By submitting to the truth of the past, you free your spirit and allow it to soar and show you the way. I have been inspired by sharing and learning from so many, and I have learned that all paths lead to our destiny.

Shedding the shame of your past allows you to move forward, feeling lighter. The past is not erased, for all that we have said and done will catch up to us, but we must accept it and deal with it one way or another.

Facing the things that we fear the most makes us take these quantum leaps in our journey. When I was nine years old, my grandmother told me that fear was a concept, that people used to control others. She said, "Fear is a lie. It doesn't exist." I remember thinking that she was kind of kooky and feeling like my whole world fell apart—everything I thought I knew was suddenly changed.

Grandma had it right. Fear is an illusion that we have created to manufacture safety in our mind. It is truly mind over matter, because there is no proof that being afraid makes us safer. You be the judge. There is a wide gap between prevention, and full blown fear.

People can suffer from many different kinds of fears, some

more severe than others. Some we are able to skip over, and some we spend our whole lives trying to avoid—or do we? Do we attack the symptom or the cause? Why are we so afraid? Perhaps we are afraid because we cannot find answers or because we do not understand our answers.

Maybe we are afraid because we cannot control what happens, and the results are unknown? No one ever said that accepting the past was easy. In fact I have found that often taking the right path is never easy. Opinions vary on the 'how' or the 'why' of the phenomenon, but we have all lived that moment when it is easier to take short-cuts, but we end up 'paying' for it later somehow. Mostly, indeed it is the unknown that we fear. Fear that we may somehow fail; Fear that we will bear the consequences of our actions; Fear that others will judge us; Fear of getting in too deep, and get stuck with no way out; Fear that we will regret our decisions in the future, etc, etc, etc.

Fear is subjective, and when you achieve a wider perspective and an open perception, it dissolves. Try it. Tackle the things, situations, or moments that keep you imprisoned in fear. Take it upon yourself to view things differently, attack the fear, and see it fully. In doing so, you are accepting your past and your limitations. Whether you succeed or fail is not important—the mere attempt is a success. Most people are 'frozen' in fear, and therefore live a limited 'version' of life, due to the fact they choose not to 'put themselves out there', in order to avoid 'drama'. But what does that really mean? Is 'Putting yourself out there' really a bad thing? Why?

Putting yourself out there can mean so many things. It can mean that you 'chose' to participate in a social, work, school, or family activity, instead of excluding yourself, or be a spectator that only observes. It can mean to be 'Pro-Active' and be the first to volunteer, help, take an assignment, give out your name, answer a question, or make a suggestion. It can mean (if you are single) that you chose to actively seek a partner, or make new friends, or be social.

As the previous statement implies, putting yourself out there can mean different things to different people. What does it mean to you?

Return to Life! An empowerment of the Spirit

You can now decide whether things in your life are acceptable, uncomfortable, or unacceptable. Your fear or that of others does not decide for you; YOU decide.

Acceptance saved my life. Does this sound like you or someone you know? Perhaps what you have experienced was not as violent, but it was traumatic all the same. The story of abuse happens every day, regardless of gender, color, nationality, sexual orientation, or religious belief. It is one that many live with and do not report or write about. Unfortunately, some do not survive.

Universal is the story of violence and bad choices that can lead you down a dark path, but even a dark path cannot keep you from finding the inner peace you seek. No violence, pain, homelessness, or despair can keep you from this peace, because once you open your perceptions, become aware, and submit to yourself, you unlock the key to becoming whole again.

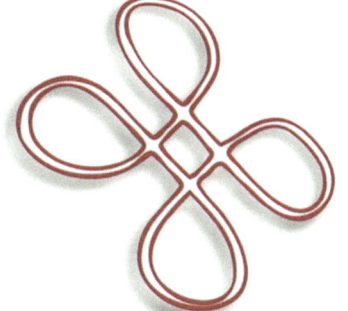

RULES OF THE GAME:
Philosophy of Self

So far, we have opened our perception and taken some steps toward becoming aware. Now we need to understand the rules to this chaos we call life.

We have been programmed through school, religion, and upbringing about certain manners and behaviors, the 'dos and don'ts' of life. We are taught to be considerate, thoughtful, honest, satisfied, content, thankful, and humble. All of this is good, but what would *good* be without *bad*? This is the game.

There must be a balance.

Ignorance is *not* bliss, it is just a programming to conform.

Not knowing, trying, questioning, or analyzing means that you are following the path of life with blinders on. How can you make a life-changing decision without knowing all the facts? By 'Impulse Shopping'?

Do not 'impulse shop' the big decisions in your life. When you have not weighed all the options, you may face disastrous consequences. Let us analyze this statement further: Say that you have a business meeting scheduled for ten o'clock tomorrow morning, and this meeting is important. Tonight, you have the opportunity to go out and stay out late with your friends. In this scenario, different types of awareness bring different results.

IMPULSE SHOPPING

You go out and party hard. The opportunity is there, it is what you desire, and you feel that you "deserve" it. The next day, you miss the meeting, are reprimanded at work, lose the client, and lose the respect of a lot of people.

THINKING IT OUT

You realize that although the opportunity is in front of you, you do not have to take it. Though you feel that you deserve it and want to go out, you can recreate the opportunity at another time. There is that meeting in the morning: What will we do about it? Will you lose the client if you do not show up? Will you lose face at work? Remember, you don't wait for things to happen, you make them happen.

You can take the following steps: You call a colleague, employee, or assistant, and tell them of the meeting or appointment to ensure that they can attend for you. You prepare the notes and agenda for the meeting and make the materials accessible to others. You go out with your friends but remain aware of the meeting in the morning. At some point, you have to decide whether you are willing to risk the embarrassment or loss of the client in exchange for the time you have set aside for yourself. If you decide that you do not want to take the risk, you call it an early evening, go home and rest, wake up fresh in the morning, and go to your meeting.

In the first scenario, you consciously make the decision to stay out and party hard, knowing the repercussions. You get home late and exhausted, call the secretary or colleague of your choice, and tell them to either take over the meeting or reschedule. Now after that whole long comparison, what is the defining factor that makes one differ from the other? This is simple: The phone call. Would you be upset about the consequences? Would you ask why?

In the second scenario, things go smoothly because of better planning. You are aware of the potential consequences, and even though you have taken precautions to avoid an unwanted outcome, if things were to not work out, you would be able to accept it, knowing that you had done all you could. It is all a matter of perception and being aware of your situation.

This scenario can be applied to an appointment, a meeting, a sales call, a client, a patient, a test or exam, etc. Whatever the situation in particular is, the lesson is the same: 'Thinking it out' *always* works best than 'Impulse Shopping' major decisions.

THE PARTS OF THE SELF

Whether it is life's buzzing, like the running around in the early morning (or the staggering around in the afternoon), as we get ready for the day, thinking of the never-ending tasks ahead that we mindlessly set up for ourselves, knowing full well that we will probably only get to about half of them, it seems that we are always running on a "default" state of being, a point of reference from which our behaviors originate. What is that part of us? Is it our personality or our persona? or both?

This subject is worth exploring. We may stop and contemplate such issues, but we fail to remain on the subject long enough to gather any concrete information. This answer requires a journey inward.

One of the main components of the *self* is in knowing where one part of you ends and another begins. Parts, you ask? Yes, parts. The self has multiple parts. We all develop many facets as we grow, and, of course, our 'whole' is always greater than the sum of our parts. We develop *personas* as we encounter situations, events, places, people, and experiences.

Think of the avatar on your social media page that reflects your mood or the 'game face' you put on before a meeting or a visit with family. These are your personas. The number and type vary from individual to individual, but the fundamentals are the same. We temporarily 'put on' these aspects of ourselves as the situation requires.

How do we know which one of our personas is the true self? What if we carried a bit of all of them in ourselves? What if we just shed these personas at the first opportunity? The questions and meditations are infinite, however only one question matters in the end: Do *you* really know who you are?

We go through life personifying who we *are* and who we *want to be*, however sometimes the two run together; sometimes they each go their own way. Our personas are interchangeable and can be manageable, but how do we keep our sanity while changing all these hats, and performing all these seemingly schizophrenic changes? This is where most people, myself included, inevitably get into trouble.

It is important to reflect not only on questions about your present but also on questions about your future. Always knowing that there is room for change, and that the present is never absolute, will become a subconscious motivator. The key to understanding this phenomenon is to tackle it head on. The main questions are "Who am I?" and "Who do I want to be?" "Who am I?" seems almost obvious and overly simplistic, but it is not.

The question triggers myriad trains of thought. Who am I at heart? What are my desires? What drives me? All these questions arise from what seems like a relatively simple inquiry.

The next fundamental question is a whopper. Are you happy with *who* you are? Really happy? If the answer is just a question mark, as it was with me, the next questions you should ask yourself are these: "Why have I chosen the persona I have? When do I use it? Why? What part about the persona I choose do I feel is of benefit? Have I ever stopped to think of possible negative side effects? Even if they are acceptable side effects, have I really considered them?" Only you can answer these questions.

These are the questions that you do not allow others to even ask or insinuate.

In my case, I developed a 'protector' persona that allowed me to survive the trials and tribulations of my early life. It was the perfect companion to the persona that felt victimized.

The main persona that took over in 'survival mode' was the angry, hurt, distrustful, and self-sufficient Krystaline. I was the same person as far as my talents, creativity, and skills... but my personality? Let's just say that it was damaged.

The problem with that, is that the benefits that were immediately experienced were positive, inasmuch as the 'success' that business brought me, as I adapted to the traits that were required to achieve this. I was tough: I stood my ground as a woman in business (a very young one). I built a reputation for producing results, and most of all I was considered an independent, no-nonsense player. As the progeny of two brilliant people, both with their own legacies, I was labeled a savant in business. It seemed great—but was it really?

Here comes the truth: At what expense do we seek success? I used to live by the saying, "Whatever it takes!" This meant success at all costs. On the surface it seemed a win-win way to live, but let me assure you that it was not. The chart below shows the pros and cons of this state of being. Use this as an example, and complete your own chart.

THE FAÇADE: A MANUFATURED PERSONALITY

Pros	Cons
Excellence in producing results *(getting what you want)*	Objectification of people, lack of empathy *(by dehumanizing them; if they are not human, they cannot get hurt)*
Satisfaction of ego	Constantly having to out-do yourself becomes exhausting
Avoiding hurt *(because you put up a wall)*	Losing touch, living in your own subjective reality
Independence	Personal isolation, living in a bubble, never allowing yourself to get too close
Constant motivation *(by way of praise or escape)*	Withdrawal, depression
Suspension of stressors *(ignoring impending problems)*	Pretending that things will get better *(ignoring them will often make things worse)*

There is a huge difference between acting on a well-informed, thought-out strategy (to please yourself, successfully conduct a meeting or event, fulfill a responsibility or prior engagement, and so on) and depending on someone else's approval of you, or your actions. The differentiation is tricky, and approval-seeking behavior has both advantages and disadvantages.

The trouble with philosophizing, analyzing, and eventually hypothesizing on the state of advantages and disadvantages of any given subject, herein being the topic of 'Approval-Seeking Behavior', is that it forces us to pass judgment, and who is to say that one person's judgment is better than another's? Who is to say that one's judgment is morally acceptable? Who's standard of morality do we use to tip the scales? What are the rules to the game?

In analyzing this subject matter in particular, I have come to several realizations, the main one being that in order to be able to mimic other's behaviors, without imminent absorption and merging, one must first find the identity and philosophy of oneself. Meaning, that before I can strive to incorporate myself into some sense of normality, as defined by the dominant polis, or societal majority, you must first know yourself and really find who you are, the person at your core—not just what shows on the surface, what is publicly shown, or your "persona."

Therefore, after much consideration, I have decided to define the topic at hand, as I see and understand it, and based on this, the following advantages and disadvantages have been concluded. To start, approval-seeking behavior is by definition the constant endurance in all things aspiring to something greater, greater in a sense of a breakthrough, better, more innovative, more inventive, and so on. It is the need to pursue the "winning recipe" in order to receive commendation. Even thinking of the affirmations is part of approval-seeking behavior.

These behaviors are with us at birth. A baby instinctively seeks its mother's approval, and her smile is a reward. A toddler is induced into good behavior with similar tactics, and as we grow older, we are conditioned to get good grades to receive approval. As adults, this behavior infiltrates our business life. Being a woman adds to the pressure. In a chiefly patriarchal society, where being equal does not mean equal treatment, greater results are expected in order to attain success and approval. So in the end my questions all arrive at the same point. Why is this bad behavior? Is it not the rules of society that dictate the norms? While the need for approval has been drilled into us all our lives, how do we deprogram ourselves? No wonder some people have a hard time adapting. It used to be that society mandated most behaviors, and then the revolution of the 60's happened, and everything changed. But things went from one extreme to another. How do we reach a happy medium?

To use myself as a quick example, I see some of my past problems being seeded in some of the reasons mentioned. I see that I have used some of the methods discussed, as I developed this protector persona. Successes due to such, can be counted as small victories in school, business, community relationships, career, and even family.

Leadership is imbued with responsibilities that demand such behaviors be undertaken. Mainstream society accepts this without further protest. How are you supposed to come to the conclusion of right and wrong? As they say… "Hindsight is 20/20," "If I knew then, what I know now"… Of course now, trying to look for the Pros and Cons becomes a matter of the judgment we spoke about, because it implies that one must look at certain things as "bad" or negative, when perhaps at one time we saw absolutely nothing wrong with anything: How do we apply what we have learned?

There are some side effects or disadvantages to the pattern. One of the main negative points is that you must constantly engage mentally, emotionally, and physically for long periods of time. This is exhausting and turns you into a 'workaholic,' leading to a multitude of ailments like sleep deprivation, poor diet, and other serious health risks. In addition to all this, there is also a funny thing that happens... When constantly seeking approval, you lose touch with what you truly aspire to reach: Other people (Like in our chart).

Objective empathy is the first thing to go, as you worry about yourself and those immediately around you. You stop asking what pleases *you*. You take on the burden of other's objectives before your own, training yourself to always please others first. This often leads to getting 'the short end of the stick' and brings on other behavioral problems by combination, or as a by-product.

Having a one-track mind of pleasing others makes the world pass you by without realizing it. You exist in a type of 'bubble' or 'waking coma' where you float over things that are of no interest (those that do not include accolades) and hover over the things that do engage us. Life goes by very quickly, and you struggle to constantly keep up. This *rat race* becomes overall exclusive, as it draws only individuals willing to do *whatever it takes*, and that also makes the lifestyle or behavior appealing. Stress constantly tightens your stomach, and tension builds in your muscles. It's not a pretty picture.

I have lived, loved, gained, and lost. In the search for myself, I have found that approval-seeking behavior is inherently linked to a view of ourselves from within. Until we learn to accept ourselves, we cannot find authentic approval from others. To reach that balance, we must come to terms with the reality of self, learn who we really are, accept the good and the bad from our past, make changes in the present, and create a new, more balanced future.

The constant search is rooted in this behavior. The trick is to know which needs you must meet and to make sure that you are *always* included in the equation. Most mistakes in life are made when we do not listen to our conscience, and whether subliminally or not, it carries weight. It is important to self-assess, asking yourself directly what your wishes are before proceeding. I have found much comfort in the fact that I have learned to consider myself the most important critic in my own life. I can dialogue and take in information without the need to "be in the driver's seat," or be in total control, so-to-speak.

The philosopher René Descartes penned my thoughts perfectly: "I am a thing that thinks, that is to say, a thing that doubts, affirms, denies, understands a few things, is ignorant of many things, wills, refrains from willing, and also imagines and senses." – Insofar as Shakespeare's phrase "to be or not to be" is not the question but is the answer. By being yourself, you leave the homogenizing to others. You realize that we are all unique human beings and that although we may mimic others, we may never replicate another's behaviors absolutely. Though individual, we are all part of a whole. Those thoughts were the fuel to my redemption, and in so thinking I welcomed my new form of being. This is who I am. I am flawed because I am human, and human is all I can ask to be.

THE CALM:
Luck has *nothing* to do with it

Sometimes it seems that the universe is trying to test you or tell you something, especially when, no matter what you do, things don't work out. It's easy to blame 'bad luck' or speak of 'the luck of the draw.' What does that mean anyways? These sayings refer negatively to events that do not fulfill your expectations; however seldom do I hear the flip side.

I think an example is in order, to help explain my point. One time, I had planned a trip for a conference. I made my reservations almost three weeks in advance, and I planned out all the tasks I needed to do before my trip.

At one point, it seemed that so many tasks needed finishing that I would not be able to make my trip. I was excited about this trip—I was a keynote speaker at this event—and did not want to miss it. All-in-all as the days passed, a certain intensity seemed to burn itself out. Although to start it did seem as though the barrage of obstacles would know no end; babysitting, work, impromptu commitments, and so on; and then, just like that, a few days before my trip, certain calm came over me. Everything just sort of fell into place.

On the day of my flight, I awoke at 6:00 a.m. I took advantage of the fact that the children were still sleeping and took a nice, hot, relaxing shower. As I packed (yes, at the last minute!) and finished up my chores, I made mental notes of everything on my checklist, and still my positive flow was going strong.

I finished my checklist: Ready the children; start to gather all the necessary things . . . oh no! It was already ten o'clock!

There was still much to do. I had to drop off the children, say goodbyes, and let us not forget, drive to the airport. By some miracle, I got myself to the airport and checked in by eleven o'clock. All seemed well, and as I confidently began to walk to the security checkpoint, I realized that I had forgotten to plan for this step: Time at the security checkpoint was my downfall.

As you may have deduced, I missed my flight. That was certain, but what was not certain was my reaction at the apparent debacle. I learned that the next flight did not leave until 4:45 p.m.; as I received the news, everything seemed to slow down and stretch forever; I felt my flow, my mojo, my luck collapse.

That moment when you make a split-second decision—when you consider all the options before you act—is worth studying, because whatever follows will affect the rest of your day. The outcomes, or realities sink in, the *what ifs'*. What if I freak out and think of all the things I could have completed? What if I had booked the later flight? Could have, should have, would have.

I could bite the bullet and deal with the situation. I was not expected until the next day at the conference, and I could still arrive in time to settle in. It was all a matter of perception and perspective. One perspective can be negative and lead to an anxiety attack, while the other can allow you to decompress and switch gears to a more positive outlook. The latter comes when you open your perception and view these moments as signals to slow down and get in sync.

And just like that, in a flash, a blink of an eye, I decided that I would remain open and aware. I took a breath and allowed myself to feel a connection within, to feel human and fallible, even if it made me vulnerable. As I exhaled, I walked past airport security and was free to relax and find something to do while I waited. I emerged from the checkpoint re-energized and ready to enjoy my experiences.

I could take in the details and the lessons that might present themselves; the simplicities. As I got the directions to my departure gate, I felt that calm come over me again, the sense that I was in the right place at the right time. Then another sensation came over me.

My stomach rumbled, begging to be fed for the first time today. This prompted me to look around, and as I visually scanned the area, my gaze stopped at the sight of a group of nicely laid out tables, in what seemed to simulate a sidewalk setting. There was certain quaintness about the place, and the semi-private feeling of the artificial shade created appealed to me.

It was a good thing that all this happened in this way, and not any other, because I wrote this chapter as I sat in this Parisian café-style ambiance. I realized that I had made a life- changing set of choices, and I was glad that things happened as they did.

In retrospect, I very much enjoyed my trip. The time I had alone, waiting for my flight, helped me to settle a lot of things in my mind. I was able to adjust and enjoy my own company. I felt centered, ready for anything, ready to deal with whatever might come next. It was a renewed sense of self-awareness and confidence.

Like a labyrinth, life takes us on so many twists and turns that we end up dizzy, distracted from our end goal. These distractions are small but many, and if you do not pay attention, gradually, there occurs a shift. A shift, that if left unchecked, will eventually divert you from your path.

It is only when we are forced into making decisions that we have the benefit of life telling us, "Is this what you really want?" We decide whether the answer is 'Yes' or 'No' and feel a renewed sense of purpose. Why is that? Why must we wait for the signals to hit us in the face, like a wall of bricks, before we react?

It holds true, that just as this experience gave me a sense of readiness that I wouldn't have gotten to experience that, had the series of events gone differently. Every piece had its part to play. It was almost as though the situation forced me to decide on the perspective that brought me the greatest benefit. In the end, isn't that the moral of the story?

WHY DO WE TELL OURSELVES LIES?

I have encountered a social experiment that I have come to call the '**Selective Amnesia**' factor. Although fully conscious of details or the lies we omit or add, we choose to temporarily believe them, and in doing so fool not the target of the lies but ourselves. This leaves us in a perpetual state of 'suspension of disbelief' and renders us vulnerable to anyone with a good story.

In essence, we live the lies of our own choosing, and we become dependent on them once we have become accustomed to having them around us. The secrets that we often label as 'skeletons in the closet' are but the truths that we have chosen to ignore.

We are like 'absentee landlords' in the bodies we inhabit, and therefore we miss the most important reasons for being. We become accustomed to being stuck in details or in denying our actions.

We remain forever glamoured by 'selective amnesia' and dream of a reality that does not exist except in our heads. We remain stuck, in limbo, floating, and *lost*. Lost, in a sea of confusion, that if we had our head on straight we would see through. If we had a greater perspective, we could find a solution; we could swim to shore.

What holds us back? Lies, fear, and conflict. The process of acceptance? The prospect of finding peace within perhaps? Are we afraid to simply let go, and allow to happen what must happen?

Are we afraid to let others down truly? Are we merely afraid of someone's negative opinion?

Is it that we empathize and wish not to hurt others with the truth behind our lies?

Is it that we fear conflict and choose not to face a reality that we fear or do not approve of?

Is this facade merely a tactic to further remain hidden from ourselves? Are we afraid to face the truth for what it is, to see life as less than perfect?

Is it that we are afraid to be who we were truly meant to be? Are we afraid to have faith in ourselves?

In a nut shell... Is it **_faith_** that we lack in ourselves?—faith in nature, faith in our fellow human being, faith in the system, faith in our family, *faith in life?*.

The number one reason that we fret and doubt, remain scared and amnesiac, is that we do not understand the *why*. Why are we here? What is our purpose? We feel we have the need to know or understand all, for knowing brings surety.

Being sure, is nothing more than faith. In the end, the answer is simple. Have a little faith that perhaps the things we do not understand were meant to be this way for now. Perhaps when the time is right, we will know the answers we seek. Perhaps if we simply ask, we shall receive? The important thing to remember is that *nothing is certain except the uncertain.*

We do not always have to have all the answers. We do not have to always understand. Our lives have meaning in the search alone.

To ignore the parts of the journey we call life because the details do not always come to you somehow seems like cheating. Bubbles are okay for protection, but remember to use them only as needed. Living in a self-protective bubble isolates you from the mission we all have: To live each day in the fullest.

The greatest gift we have is the experience of waking up each day and taking in the beauty that surrounds us in addition to the pain and sorrow. Our experience of life is dependent on all its aspects, not just the ones we choose.

MONEY, HEALTH and LOVE

Our true self emerges as layers are peeled away, one by one. The more you get to the center of yourself, the more you see the real you. In good times, it seems that we all have the ability to be pleasant and wonderful to others. In bad times, we all have the potential to throw "low blows." So how do we go for the middle? It all depends on our way of looking at things and, like anything else, how we process events.

They say that you never really know a person until you are forced to live with them for more than just a few days. In my experience, this holds true, I once thought I *knew* my counterpart, and in the end, after having lived together, I found out otherwise.

I once asked a very special friend, "What do you seek from life?" He answered, "Money, Health and Love. Those are the things that make the world go 'round." This got me thinking. Without one, the other two seem out of balance, and all three do seem to be what most people seek, when you get down to it.

People say that '**Money**' cannot buy happiness, even I can testify to that, but I can say that it can certainly make life comfortable.

'**Health**' alone cannot pay the bills or put food on the table, but it can give you the time and energy to do something that will.

And '**Love**'! Love is the twenty-million-dollar question. Love is the fundamental part of our being; it is probably the only force that *can* make the world go around. Love is the powerful emotion that can influence our happiness, our self-esteem, and all our relationships. Love can nurse you back to health; and love, they say, transcends time and space.

With all of these benefits, what is love? And how do I get it? The simple four-letter word has been misunderstood, chopped down, tagged, and categorized. It is compartmentalized and targeted to a moment or a specific meaning (Platonic, romantic, sibling, parental, and so on). Why can it not all just be *love*? Can it be defined as a feeling of mutual sentiment, appreciation, well-being, peace, and balance felt toward a person, animal, object, place, or activity?

The euphoria of love comes from surrendering to the moment, letting your guard down, and allowing yourself to be vulnerable. In this state of pure acceptance, you can soak in the object of your affections. So it is true that we all seek the thrill of love, but we do not want to be exposed, even if for a short time. This is the main reason that people are afraid to fall in love, take the plunge, or even say the words "I love you."

Without diminishing the meaning of saying "I love you" should not be avoided for fear of future commitments attached to the words. I have loved, basked in the glow of it, and later felt different. That is okay. Even if it is only for a moment, a brief interlude, the experiences recorded in your memory will be with you forever, whether you build on them or not. To say "I love you" does not imply any kind of exclusivity. It simply means *now, this, here, you, me*—that is all.

Human love is what it is. I imagine that if there are other intelligent beings in the universe, our ability to love is probably what makes humans unique. Love does not need a label or a disclaimer. Love stands alone or enhances other attributes (like health and money), so these three together do indeed seem to make a perfect combination. What it boils down to is our search for each other. We want the joy of making the connections, touching and being touched, loving and being loved. I have had moments of open love and then had a moment of awkwardness, wondering if I had made a mistake. We should not be afraid to enjoy a moment, touch others' lives, or allow others to touch ours, even if with a perfect stranger.

To share those moments, you have to give yourself completely, and most people do not verbalize it for fear of reciprocity. What if I say the words, and then they are taken too seriously? What if this person does not feel the same? So you leave yourself in a 'Catch 22'-- *damned if I do, and damned if I don't*.

Why not share a moment because you want to? You are responsible only for your own assumptions and can only answer for yourself. At the end of the day, showing love for someone, something, or someplace—because you want to and not expecting anything back—enables you to live the moment fully. If you take and apply this concept to other roadblocks, you will find that health and money will surely follow.

So how can stating the obvious change the past? Fear comes from the act of being selfish. With the act of wanting certain future moments to occur, the fear that others will not see things as you do, that people will change their feelings about you or those you love, and on, and on, and on—we hold ourselves in a cage of our own design.

All we really need in life is to live in the present, appreciate the past, and look forward to the future. To deny ourselves the things we seek is a diversion that often takes us off course from our path. If we truly want to achieve happiness we need to shed our fears and accept situations as they come. **What is** and what '***might be***' are two different things. Without being open to them, how will you know '***what will be***'?

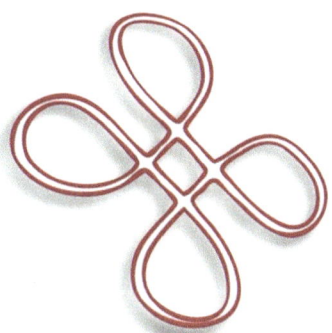

BALANCE & CHANGE

The delicate balance that is the dance of interpersonal relationships, is a complicated task to accomplish, especially when you have been absent from someone's life and then re-enter it. It is almost as if you are meeting for the first time. Memories of the old behaviors or characteristics remain and therefore influence the future of the relationship.

Relationships can mean friendship, family, or even romantic. In either case, the outcome of assumptions is the same. How do we live down our past? Be it good or bad, the past seems to be something that we are 'stuck with' and cannot 'shake' no matter how much we improve or change. People can blind themselves when they do not want to acknowledge any changes: It is a common occurrence, and often a frustration we just *accept* and say to ourselves "That is just how that person is"—Do we really accept this?

The answers lay in the eyes of the beholder. How do you view things? Other people's perceptions, for the most part, never seem to be related to the present. They see the ghost of the persona of your past, they do not see these are the actions of now, not those of yesterday.

We are who we are, and we sometimes discover new parts of ourselves that we didn't even know were there. We are constantly changing, and because of that, anyone who expects people to always be the same will almost certainly be disappointed.

It is said that the more things change, the more they stay the same. The world, or the environment around us, does not change as rapidly, or as dramatic as we think. Instead, it is we who change dramatically as we learn and grow, as we absorb and adapt. Our context, our view, changes, and therefore the landscape that surrounds us changes. Think of a movie that you watched as a child and watched again as an adult. It is the same movie but a different view. The meanings, ideas, and interpretations you now find in the movie were certainly not there before. Or were they?

In the same way, why would a living, breathing person remain unchanged? The sayings 'people don't change' and our recent discussion topic converge and come to mean the same thing. It all depends on us. 'people don't change' is often an opinionated stand point, taken to mean that no matter how much a person learns or grows, he will always be the same.

Seemingly, these two different ways of contemplating the point seem to be in eternal conflict. Are they? What if people do not change? What if we are all born with a blueprint of potential? What if, based on parameters that include our life choices, the decisions we make and the actions we follow, we are opening or exposing a different part of ourselves?

We are all born with a road map, and as we go along in life, we keep discovering exciting and new ways to read and interpret this map. The more we learn, the better we are able to understand its directions, explore new destinations, and decide whether or not to change paths. The map is vast and filled with myriad possibilities.

If the map (blueprint) does not change, then people don't change—or do they? Perhaps we do change, and even though the landscape around us seems to remain the same, like an ancient ruin waiting for us to catch up on our knowledge in order to understand its secrets, we do absorb the experiences we encounter, and inevitably we are changed, whether we like it or not. That the more we travel, we see, we hear, we taste, we live and we interact with others, the more we add to our endless repertoire of experiences, traits, and behaviors.

Maybe we do all of the above... and the new parts of ourselves are as much a part of us as the old parts. Maybe we just keep improving and should be proud of the past. Part of balance is acceptance, and the first step to accept is ourselves, all of ourselves. Could it be that others then *do* see changes in us, they just choose not to acknowledge it? Finding balance is about the search for truth within ourselves.

Discovering ourselves is a lifelong adventure, and your journey is yours alone. Once you accept this, you can respect others' journeys. Under this line of thought, then we can safely say that another's journey is not your own, so that tolerance is born of this mutual respect.

Balance is accepting '***yourself***' first and *then* accepting others. To do so, fears must be turned to serenity and anxieties into wisdom. It is in the 'not knowing' that we commit most of our mistakes and atrocities. In *ignorance* live the fears and the judgments that keep the blinders on. How can we be better if we never know who we really are? How can we love others if we do not love ourselves?

We mistake the 'pleasing' of others for pleasing ourselves. Because we often seek acceptance from others first (which is the opposite of balance), we remain entangled in desperate actions: It may be a parent, friend, sibling, significant other, your child, the neighbor, the pets, etc... It is this fundamentally backward thinking that takes us downhill.

Life—our road map—has a funny way of finding balance. There are always signs: A single word, or a moment of sheer epiphany might be right in front of us; We just have to pay attention to them.

Balance, as a whole, always happens. The scales are tipped one way or the other. Keep your eyes open, take in all that you encounter, seek within, and find yourself. In the end, being lost is as beneficial as being found. The faith within should always burn strong, because we have no enemies as strong as ourselves. We are our only demise. Tragedy, pain, sadness, despair, and hate are insignificant compared to the damage we can inflict on ourselves.

Know that as long as you have **_faith_** in yourself, there is nothing beyond your reach. Finding it is easy, but keeping it burning strong—that is a real labor of love. Are you ready to start?

RAINBOW OF LIFE (Second Edition)

Just as in life, where nothing is what it seems, so too is the Rainbow a box of gifts. Rainbows in general are a beautiful thing to experience: A thing of wonder that fills the mind with imagination. Rainbows are but another expression, and perfect example, of how perception can alter what we see.

The idea of a rainbow has existed for as long as we have had a collective human memory; perhaps still even longer than that, and that is why we hold it so vividly as a concept, or an idea, rather than a 'thing' or an 'object'. What I mean is, when we look at a rainbow, immediately a 'feeling' comes to the very forefront of our being. The rainbow is a perfect example for me to describe all the philosophies in this book, and in so doing it perfectly illustrates this point, both metaphorically and physically.

A rainbow is a barrage, a shower of emotions and conscious actions—manifested as a reaction to surrounding phenomena. Thus, it can be said that a rainbow therefore, can be experienced not only through the common physical senses, but also through our psychic sense, that is to say the sense that it touches our very being psychologically and emotionally.

I have seen people experience a multitude of emotions, almost immediately after witnessing this phenomenon: The rainbow.

But what is a rainbow? Is it a symbol of Unity or Individuality? Or both? The real question should be, I would guess: What does a 'rainbow' mean to you?

R.Krystaline Carbajal

[*Please stop a moment to observe and write*]

IN THIS PHOTOGRAPH, WHAT DO YOU SEE?

Observations/Meaning to You: _____

_____

_____

_____

I will tell you a recent story that helps to convey my thoughts on this... It was 5:00 am, and I had to wake everyone in the house to get ready for our long journey ahead. I had many tasks to complete before leaving (as usual), including packing some lunch, as appointments all day, and a limited budget and time, would keep us on the road most of the day.

As everyone is running around, doing last minute checks for things needed on our road trip and loading and un-loading the car is going on in the background, my husband spoke loudly above the bustle and said "If we don't hurry up and leave now, we are not going to make our first stop on time." Mind you, the atmosphere is already tense, between the cooking for eating, packing the lunch, the readying of all bags, packing of sweaters and coats, and yes, don't forget the drizzle outside that is quickly turning into a light rain—it was almost insanity!... and then, there it was! A big thundering sound, just as the last word left my husband's mouth warning us to hurry up.

Prompted by the sense of urgency provided by the 'sound off' of the thunder, we all—after a brief pause—gathered into our travel positions in the vehicle, and rushed off to the road that leads to the highway. Just as the last person was getting in, we hear a 'clink' on the hood and the windows.

The scattered 'clinks' turned into 'thumps', and as we got to the main road, a big whopping 'thud' hit the roof top so loud that it made everyone jump and laugh at how goofy we all looked when we got startled.

And then just like that, the 'clinks', 'thumps', and 'thud' disappeared. The road ahead was clear. Not even a drizzle! It was like we passed and cleared a storm cloud. Pretty soon someone in the back of the vehicle said loudly and excited... "Look! A rainbow!" We stopped the car, and as the driver, I could see the rainbow emerging from the darkest clouds, through the side mirror. It was amazing. Then, just as sudden and mysterious as it appeared, it disappeared, but not before putting a smile on everyone's face.

As the day went on, we all settled in for the long ride. Our first stop would not be for two hours. That first stop was the longest. All-in-all, after numerous bathroom breaks, appointments, pit-stops, and errands were completed; after a packed lunch had been devoured, we then made our way back home and decided at the last minute, to make one last stop at the grocery store, before taking on the last hour of our trip home (yes, we live in a very remote area).

Exhausted, but satisfied that we had accomplished all we had set out to do, we all took a much needed break, also good to stretch our legs a bit.

Remember that anytime there are long road trips, and there are several people (of all ages) crammed into a vehicle, there are bound to be tensions building. Add to that the fact that you tend not to eat as well, while on the road then you would at home, and add to that the multiple personalities, likes and dislikes all together, confined into one small space, and you get an immediate brew of mixed emotions that could turn out to be quite stressful... for everyone!

So just as we all got a chance to press our 'Pause Button', and take a breath of fresh air in relief, we all looked up at the sky at different times... and there she was, a DOUBLE RAINBOW!

The significance of this story might seem banal, or out of sorts: boring with useless details. However, this story carries an important question, why do rainbows make us smile? It is fair to also note other people's reaction to rainbows in this story. While admiring the rainbows in awe and wonderment, I noticed that everyone walking about in the parking lot, on that cold, rainy, dark and gloomy day, no one was looking at their surroundings, much less up into the sky! It goes along with people walking about in this almost 'waking sleep' or 'auto-pilot' mode. Walking from their cars to the store, barely looking at one another, looking down at a cell phone the whole way, even on the edge of zombie mode, people were automatons.

This behavior, of living in this self-inflicted 'bubble', goes hand-in-hand with people's lack of import as to one's appearance (i.e. leaving home and going to the store in bunny slippers and pajama pants).

Can you imagine the 'zombie' epidemic we at hand? Nowadays even my 20 month old fights me for my smartphone or tablet, to play games or mostly watch videos. What's up with that? I don't remember craving remote controls or phones when I was a child. Imagine my amazement when I am pondering these questions and philosophies in my head as I am looking onto the automatons in the parking lot, and get snapped out of my thought cloud when my 20 month old yells loudly, "Look! Bainbow." Almost immediately people at random heard her shout in excitement (like over a loud speaker), as if the mere word 'rainbow' (so cutely expressed by the toddler as 'bainbow') suddenly 'activated' everyone, like something internal switched on and snapped them out of their stupor.

It was amazing to see this incident work like magic. As if it was a 'code word' that triggered an 'awakening' or 'awareness' buried within. An amazing thing took place: A Rainbow!

I sat there in my vehicle, with the door open, watching and observing as one by one people started looking up at the sky. Soon, others would look up too, and then the pointing at the sky started, followed by multiple chatter amongst perfect strangers, the topic being, 'Did you see the rainbow?'

Even people pre-occupied on their mobile phones either stopped to take a picture and share, or while on the phone speaking with someone paused to look up and expressed the visual treat in front of them to whomever they were talking on the phone to. Overall the expression was 'Look! A Rainbow.' Needless to say, it was a jewel of a moment that turned quickly from a 'private sign' from my higher power personally for me, to the very pleasant result of a huge social experiment.

As with the epiphany that perhaps a scientist will have while discovering a break-thru, I too felt this effect in realizing that the cure to this 'zombie like' epidemic in society was carried out within nature itself, whom usually carries all the cures for our ailments of the human condition; spiritual, emotional, and physical.

The question I begged to answer was, how can something so simple as a rainbow carry such power of change and give strength of spirit? I myself was having an overwhelming and stressful day that seemed endless.

I am sure that my face acquired extra lines on that day, and yet the magnificence, and the sight of the rainbows melted all of that away. How? Why? It was amazing medicine to experience en masse. To this day, even having multiple doctors in my family; experiencing healing of all sorts personally, bearing witness to amazing and miraculous recoveries, such as my own, visiting with alternative healers: Shamans, Indigenous Medicine Men and Women, Folk Healers, Priests and Priestesses from multiple regions of the world, Wise Men and Women whom heal with prayer and/or laying-of-the-hands (sobadores/massage with prayer); I even experienced mass meditation and mass prayer in a very large group/crowd, and even after all that... This experience was UNIQUE.

So why then do rainbows appear to some people more than to others? Is it that they simply take more time to look? While others more than likely do not engage looking up at the heavens, therefore do not see as many rainbows? What about fleeting rainbows, or pick-a-boo rainbows? The ones that disappear as quickly as they appear, are they there only for a short time, long enough for the right person to see them?

Of all the phenomenon in the sky, why are we awestruck by the rainbow? Why is it the most spectacular? Why is it like a work of art? Because it is.

Honestly, I had never seen with my own eyes a double rainbow. Many rainbows I have been blessed to see-- and in these recent years I have been blessed with many--I had, of course, always experienced the almost instant smile, which I interpret as medicine for the spirit, a sort of healing energy, but again, I never experienced this particular event among a mass of people. In this line of thought I began to ask myself, how could this be? Why do these colors and 'arch' formation incite such primal reaction? What kind of 'encoding' is there within? How or why is it triggered by the sight of this phenomenon?

Although other spectacular natural phenomenon occur in our earthly skies (i.e. Aurora Borealis), the rainbow is the most spectacular, by far, and unique in its own right. Although we do not have time here in this book to go quite into depth as I would like on rainbows, it is important enough to use this example, and add this chapter to the second edition of this book. Rainbows can be captivating, mysterious, and elusive at the same time. The rainbow can signal a 'calm after the storm', or impending disasters to come.

Spiritually, rainbows carry some people's prayers and wishes up to the heavens, and for some the rainbow serves as the bridge to an afterlife, or higher spiritual realms at mortal life's end. The cohesive and collective nature of the colors of the rainbow have been taken by the human consciousness to symbolize a unity across colors and cultures to stand united and strong, while to others the individuality with which each color resonates and shines through, although next to another equally beautiful apparition, means strength and uniqueness.

None-the-less, all colors of the rainbow are uniquely beautiful, viewed on their own, or as a whole. Without one, there would not be the other. All colors must stand together, though they might not all appear together all at once. Scientifically, the colors become more fascinating and thereby adds another philosophical and spiritual level to the rainbow: There are more than one million colors present in the rainbow, some of which are not visible by the 'normal' human eye. There are rare individuals called 'tetra-chromats' that have special genetic mutations, which render an individual able to perceive more than 100 million colors, which is 10 times more than the normal eye.

Can you imagine the spectacle of color viewable for those individuals while they stare at a rainbow? Perception and awareness, or willingness to submit, has a lot to do with how we 'view' the outside world, as we have discussed so far.

This discussion, in essence, is the philosophical equivalent argument, posed by human beings since the times of Aristotle, as to the perception of the rainbow being equal to, in fact one's perception of life, as it is all dependent on a combination of outside factors beyond our control (i.e. Sunlight and Water), and then some very controllable factors like our actions and reactions to these circumstances (the reflection/refraction of light).

Therefore, although a rainbow—a perfect balance and intricate recipe for beauty and perfection—can be achieved under very rare situations filled with pre-conditions, **_IT IS POSSIBLE!_**

And so in life, as a matter of how we perceive our surroundings, and our choices, should we choose to fulfill our destiny to achieve that balance, as the rainbow has, we too must submit to some rules of the game, that once met may allow us to express our spiritual spectrum in the same splendor and magnificence as the rainbow.

THE PURPOSE OF PRAYER

To paraphrase Ludwig Feuerbach (an underrated and sadly almost forgotten great thinker): ". . . that divine wisdom is human wisdom; that the secret of theology is anthropology; . . . The necessary turning-point of history is therefore the open confession, that the consciousness of (the divine) is nothing else than the consciousness of the species; that man (as a species) can and should rise only above the limits of his individuality . . . that there is no other essence which man can think, dream of, imagine, feel, believe in, wish for, love and adore as the absolute, than the essence of human nature itself."

In this statement, all the topics we have discussed become clear. All that we search for outside ourselves has always been *inside*.

The truth we seek is buried within... in the tangled web of lies and illusions we set up for ourselves. We are all individuals, but we are part of a whole—a human consciousness or collective: The human race.

Nothing we do, say, or try to distract ourselves with, fake happiness or not, can ever outdo or compare to the satisfaction, love, and bliss found as part of the human whole. Understanding this principle will set you free.

DO NOT TAKE MY WORD FOR IT...
TRY THIS OUT YOURSELF.

When you have finished this book, re-read it. Meditate on the words. Build on them, and find within yourself the answers that you seek.

WRITTEN BY RUTH CARTER (UNITY)

This letter was written by a dear and enlightened sister in the light who has committed herself to working with women incarcerated in prison. Her questions to me and my responses follow below.

Krys:

"I have been having a dilemma about one of the girls (at a federal prison) that just recently had surgery for colon cancer. She was due to go home on August 23, and now she has been told that she cannot go home because the half-way house will not let take her, due to the fact that she needs extensive chemotherapy.

She may be transferred to a prison medical facility. So, needless to say she is very upset, as was I when she told me 'I truly had myself believing that I was going to go home and take the chemo pills.' Now a lot of people were praying for her, and I just couldn't wrap my head around why she could not co-create that for herself, because if we create with our thoughts words and deeds, then what happened?

If in fact love, hate, and desire are the emotions that create, then I am sure that she had the desire to create that for herself. Okay, let's say destiny is the reason we can't change things, or her sponsoring thought before she came into the physical world was to have cancer, or maybe her karma called for her to experience this. Then if our lives are based only on destiny why pray, meditate, etc.?

I think we pray because prayer makes us feel good, it gives us peace of mind, so it is worth it for that alone, because we all want peace of mind. So then where does co-creation fit in? Oh yes, and then there is the little thing called free will. These were just some of my questions. I pondered these for the last few days.

At center stage is free will. Let's say that we have our destiny, but we use our free will to choose which path we are going to take to fulfill that destiny. Man can overcome any limitation, because he created it by his own actions in the first place, and because he possesses spiritual resources.

How will we react to the chemistry of our returning karma? Will we accept 'responsibility' and learn the lessons of the past? or will we fall back into the same patterns? How we answer those questions will determine our destiny. It must mean how we move through the lessons that we ourselves have put before us from past lives or whatever the soul wanted to learn. Depending on how we move through the lessons is how we are *co-creating* our life.

If we accept every lesson, and with love, peace and harmony then come, we do not have to experience the same lessons, and by doing that we have co-created our lives. As far as doing good deeds and praying for others, we do that to give ourselves peace of mind and to lessen our karma. That is where the grace of goodness comes in, the more good we do, the less harsh our karma will be.

Like for example, if we really deserved to die a painful death, let's say by fire, then maybe we will just burn our finger because of the good deeds we have done, that is what is called the grace of goodness. What do you think? I'm troubled, and I need to hear your words."

Love,
Unity

MY RESPONSE TO UNITY'S LETTER

Unity,

I liked your letter on co-creation, and free will for that matter, when it comes to our destiny, but you forget that all paths lead to our creator. So whether we get distracted, entertained, hurt, or lost, eventually what is, will be.

If it is this person's destiny and karma to experience this colon cancer, and the delay for her arrival at home has placed itself in front of her, and if all other avenues to prevent this fact, court motions, appeals, grievances, etc., have been exhausted, then it must be so. What is to learn from this experience? Only she can know.

So then the paradox of prayer and meditation come to play. Why do so? If our destinies and karma have been chosen and written by us, before incarnation, what then? Why pray? Why meditate? Why heal? The answer is simple: not to "feel better," not to "prevent," not to "distract," and certainly not to waste time, but instead to not only find peace, but to find enlightenment. Praying, meditating, channeling, seeking, ceremony, these are all calls to our original primal home, our beacon of light: Our connection to ourselves and our creator, to download the original directive, the plan, the road-map. To find answers, therefore seeking the external becomes autogenous within the self.

Why must will be, will be? Because it must be so! Someone asked me the other day, "Then why is there death without reason? Why are children and babies being shot by gang-bangers or drive-bys when they did nothing to deserve that?" My answer is because it was supposed to be so, because we cannot pretend to sit and understand it all. To even try darkens our soul. It is the source of revenge and vengeance. It is the evil or dark part of our mind that seeks an answer to all problems and questions, especially those that we do not understand.

I am not saying that we should accept injustices or pardon evil deeds, much less that we should stand idle and let these events go unnoticed or have a death be in vain. But what I am saying is that there are certain things that we can control, and those we simply cannot. For those things that we cannot, no matter how hard we try, we must seek the lesson in it and learn from it. Learn to do better on the next occasion, learn to better the people around us, learn to better ourselves.

A child learns from its mistakes. That is the primary programming and great gift that our creator has given us, the *free will* to fall and fall again until we find our balance, to pick ourselves up and learn to walk. That is to be human. To evolve, we *must* make mistakes, for without them, we could not have compassion, and love, and unity. For those injustices, illness, plagues, financial ruin, solitude, and death bring us closer as a race, as a whole. It makes those who listen and *learn* stand up and use their free will. It causes great human kind movements like the equality of race and gender, civil rights, independence from tyranny, you name it. That is part of the lesson to be had.

Without an illness, there is no cure. Without a problem, there is no ingenuity to resolve. In this great process of evolution, we become more aware of our surroundings, and in this we vibrate at a higher level.

If we cannot embrace *empathy*, then we cannot be human. Human is not a state of being, it is a state of mind. Why do we call actions inhuman, inhumane, we say that a person "is not human"?: Because we must possess empathy to be able to place ourselves in someone else's shoes. That is the base of faith.

Return to Life! An empowerment of the Spirit

Why do people not understand and say, "Why would the creator allow this?" Because they do so out of lack of empathy. If you are enlightened, then you must be able to empathize and place yourself in the creator's role, co-create, and "see," understand the bigger picture. That is co-creation, not wishful thinking, not fantasy and hope, as faith is commonly misunderstood, for selfish results. Prayers are answered when one "listens" and understands what must be, must be. That is the only way to explain it. Faith is *confidence in self*.

Why must we have the "end times" before we may have peace? Why must there be war? Why must there be mass death? Why must our Mother Earth suffer the consequences of our own actions? Because *we must learn*. As children do when they fall, so we must learn from our mistakes. These events do not happen to us, we are happening to the world. We placed the sequence, the chain reaction that started this turmoil, into play, and so we must experience the consequences. It is the only way the masses will understand.

What is our duty as enlightened ones? To bear witness and help the learning process, to make others aware, to point out the times of learning from our mistakes, to decipher the lessons that must be taken from all this chaos, to restore the balance once more, and to lead the way down the path of light and love.

This is our duty—to be beacons, to be guides. We are not here to change the course of the destiny that has been set in motion before we even incarnated. Even Jesus tried and failed, but did he? Did he really fail? Did Buddha fail? Did Mother Teresa and Gandhi fail? Did the Tibetan monks, and the Krishna monks, and the Yogis and the Medicine Men, the Shamans and the Druids and the Maya priests fail? No. They did not. They led the way and accepted their destinies, no matter how bloody and how tragic, because they knew they would play an important part that would be remembered by some. And that was good enough. For if they had failed, we would not invoke their names while we ponder: What is the way?

The Incas and the Mayas knew, because of destiny and what they called communication with their creator and their surroundings, when their time would end. They knew to watch for the signs, and they accepted it with open arms, even when they knew that they would perish. So did the Native Indigenous Tribes of North America, India, and China. The time is ours to do what we must. Our time as the "present" civilization has come to an end. The time for enlightenment comes and waits for no one. And so, we must lead the way. As the saying says, "We have nothing to fear but fear itself." For all this is but an illusion, and the real light and love await us in the days to come, when the human race as a whole, and as a collective steps into it.

Lucky are those whose spirit has been freed of the tortures in the mortality of life. The baby that was killed in the drive-by shooting, the masses that drowned in a tsunami, those who died in an earthquake, those were all spirits that were called into the light. Our personal and meager troubles, our bickering and dilemmas, are insignificant in comparison with the trials and tribulations to come.

Survival of our humanity depends on our ability to *learn* from all this and "tune in" to vibrate at the creator's frequency. To find the light within and give-in to it—that is to be enlightened. That is to be human.

Light and Love always...
Krys

MEDITATIONS:
On the Journey

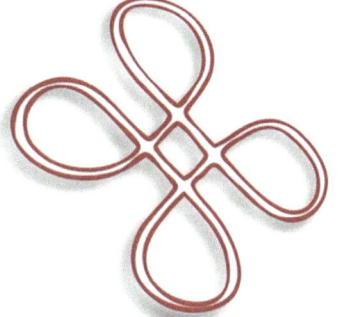

Seek your own path. Seek your own future. Create your own reality. Life is for the taking. You are not alone. Even those of us strapped in a seat as leaders, looking to imbue to future generations with more confidence and self-learning than ourselves, those of us committed to effacing the hate, jealousy, rage, and despotism inherit in the poison of society, even we get bogged down and disillusioned. We too are human, and the cure lies in all of us, in the faith we have in each other.

Tolerance and love for the organism as a whole is the end game. Within all of us lie dormant abilities of immense power. Underselling yourself further tightens the grip that the blinders you wear have on you. Liberate yourself from the self-inflicted prison you have kept yourself in, and step outside for a moment: Breathe in the air, as if it were the first time. Enjoy the sunrise or the sunset that dances for you and lingers on only long enough for you to meditate on the scenery of colors and hues it left behind.

Touch a person's life, even if it is only to help them across the street, or give them the right of way. Wear a smile every day, whether you think you have a reason for one or not, make it a habit. Start a journal, and faithfully write your experiences and your perceptions; you will be surprised at the insight you gain from reviewing these journals, you get to know yourself.

Perform the relaxation exercise as often as you feel comfortable, and soon it will be a daily routine. You will *feel* the benefits and find yourself more focused. Become aware of your surroundings. Watch and listen for a change. See what you have been missing while driving with blinders on.

Make visible, yet gradual changes in your life. At first you will need all your intentions to alter your current flow, until eventually these things come naturally. Do things like recycling, volunteering, carpool, take public transportation once in a while, best of all walk. Do things that connect you to a purpose, whichever you choose. Make a difference, and *really live* that life. This is what people sometimes refer to as *a glow,* one that people get when they feel such connection.

We are not blank canvases. Instead, we carry all this knowledge in our being. Just as plants know to seek the light, and animals instinctively know how to seek shelter, we too inherited these benefits as well, we just suppress them. We add to this database with experiences we take in, and then think we started from scratch. This is why no one will ever decipher the secrets of any one particular person's existence, because the key is yours alone to hold.

Take a chance, and get to know yourself. I can guarantee that you will be pleasantly surprised. When you see the best in yourself, then you can begin to see that same thing in others. Will you not join us?

ABOUT THE AUTHOR:
R.Krystaline Carbajal (Al-Shalaldeh)

Krystaline's Vision is to empower each individual to shape their own destiny and activate their inner strength, by the power of perception, and thereby change, improve, and build on your personal path & goals. She's is very passionate about her work, due to her own journey as a survivor of domestic violence, a permanent disability, cancer, and severe fibromyalgia.

R.Krystaline Carbajal

She often holds herself as an example of someone that had given up completely and Returned to Life!

Author, writer, speaker/lecturer, artist, musician, former member of the press, self-empowerment expert, life-coach, teacher, student, victim rights advocate, civil rights activist, and spiritual being: Krystaline fuses personal experiences with those of many whom have touched her life, and returns to the public the lessons learned from these. It is these philosophies that have been adapted, and then are presented in a way that they may apply to anyone, of any age. It is a message of Hope in Love, Faith, and Human Kind as a whole.

Krystaline has been conducting lectures and workshops since 2002, and holds multiple degrees in business, marketing, public relations, rhetoric & writing, and certifications like CDVC (Certified Domestic Violence Counselor). Krystaline continues to stay involved in business, builds new relationships wherever she goes, and offers programs to the public by cultivating partnerships with non-profit and community organizations, as well as local business to help further the cause for expansion of the Human Consciousness worldwide thru Starlight Projects Foundation, a 501(c)3 Charity.

Return to Life! An empowerment of the Spirit

All proceeds and profits of the sale of any books, lectures, workshops, appearances, events, and any and all merchandising related to Return to Life! Series goes to charity to further this work.

--"Since the moment I was told I would not walk again, I began my journey by starting at the deepest levels of my darkness. I took the inner voyage through all the doors, and emerged in the brightness of light and love that life offers us all. "

--R.Krystaline Carbajal

To learn more about Krystaline and her work visit:
www.KrystalineVisions.org **-and-** www.StarlightProjects.org

Mobile sounds and colors. Beautiful landscapes as far as the eye can see. Suddenly paintings that seemed exaggerated, somehow seem now muted.

The American Southwest and it's natural splendor leave one humbled and pensive as to our place in this world. Perspective suddenly changes encased in other beauty. Sanctuary.

Urban life seems mundane, daily tasks no longer relevant. A strange connection, a call, a whisper, a vibration. Silent is the wind as you hear it's song. Season's change in the moment to their own rhythm.

Yellow, red and rich hues of Brown. Green, blue and sprinkles of white. At sunset the hues resonate the dreams of the day. At sunset a prism entangles the rainbow and the inspirations left behind by the day. And as the benevolent light of the midwife of humanity glows, the azure hues that surround her bring out her splendor, her light dances on the mirrors of the land, and the essence of its people.

With the known as your guide, the unknown imminently becomes one's treasure.
The belly button of the world, the vortex in the land, the omniscience of the gnosis that we are one.

United, and in harmony, takes the spirit forward and gives the longing to connect.
Bubbles that float, the firmament dancing, testimony to the greatness that lies beneath.

Mother, Gia, Tierra... reminders of the heartbeats and the flow. To dream, to think, to see, to feel, to be as one. This the beginning, of the review of previous notions, the start of a journey, the end a plan.

-R.KRYSTALINE CARBAJAL
Midwife of Humanity, *a poem*

Krystaline Al-Shalaldeh

RAINBOW OF LIFE! – NEW Book Preview

A rainbow scientifically is explained through environmental phenomenon, as a cause and effect, matter of fact occurrence: Rainbows are the combination of both reflection and refraction (bending) of sunlight at a precise angle through a droplet of water. It is precise to say that rainbows cannot exist without the presence of both sun and water. The pre-existing conditions needed in order to see a rainbow are quite complex: First, there must be water present in the atmosphere, whether it be rain, mist, fog, etc., water droplets must be present in the air; Second, the sunlight must enter the water droplet at precisely 42 degrees in order for the light spectrum to be 'visibly' reflected, and then bounced off and refracted (bent) off of the water droplet's surface, causing the colors to manifest upon exiting the droplet; Third, while the sun must be BEHIND the viewer, the rain (water) must be in FRONT, in order for the rainbow to be observed. Even 'Moonbows'— Rainbows seen at night—are due to this phenomenon since the moon reflects the sunlight, because it has no light of its own. Most moonbows therefore appear when the moon is full and bright in the sky. Truly a rare event.

It is an interesting thing to note the origins, as far back as we know in our pre-history, of the images/words that describe the rainbow. As far as I was able to find, in my recent research, aborigine tribes of Australia, as far back as 6,000 years ago (archeologically dated <insert reference>) left traces of their own wonderment of the rainbow phenomenon in the form of cave paintings symbolizing the sacredness of the symbol of creation (See image below).

Ancient Australian cave drawing: A depiction of the Rainbow Serpent, known in Kakadu as Garranga'rreli, all powerful and associated with water.

In Spanish, the word for Rainbow is Arco-Iris (Arch of Iris). Iris means Rainbow or 'Eye of Heaven' in ancient Greek; to them Iris was a Goddess whom functioned as a messenger for the gods, to humanity. She was tasked with carrying the waters from the Styx (The River of Oaths) to Mount Olympus. She would receive orders from deities in the 'Eye of Heaven' and used the rainbow as her bridge to earth, where she would appear to mortals in human form with a dress 'blazing with color' that trailed behind her.

In Mexico, there are several native stories that are passed down by word of mouth still, one of them is the story of the 'Man of the 7

Colors.' As the story goes, there was an extremely poor and humble man, that did not have any money to even dress himself at all. He was a good man, that never bothered anyone, and loved to see people smile. One day, he heard the tale of a deity that had enormous power, and so he decided to go ask for help. On a day that there was a big storm, he traveled to the center of it, since the deity's power was that of thunder. He told the supernatural being his dilemma so sincerely, that he felt compassion for him and the innocence in which he asked of him this favor, and so the Thunder Being answered to him: "Although my power is great, I cannot give you any money, but I can give you another gift. I can give you the gift of 7 colors that you can use always after I come and go. With these colors you can cover your body from head to toe, but you can also make people smile at the sight of their beauty as well." And so the Man of the 7 colors is often seen after a rain, happy at the delight to make people smile, as he covers himself in the 7 colors of the rainbow, and arches his back over the land in order to see people smile at the sight.

In Hopi Native American Tradition, the rainbow is traditionally thought of as a 'Blessing' from the ancestors. The ancestors, which use the rainbow as a 'bridge' or 'portal' to visit us and impart their wisdom, visit us via this beautiful phenomenon and impart wisdom to us in order to help us along our 'Spiritual Path'. Traditionally the rainbow is seen as something that touches a person's life more often if they are seen as a 'special' person that has been chosen to receive certain 'wisdom' for healing. Medicine

Rainbow of Life! – NEW Book Preview

Men and Women are also traditionally chosen by the ancestor spirits, by having an 'extraordinary' experience (i.e. Being struck by lightning, followed by rain or rainbows, etc.)

In Hawaiian ancient beliefs, like in Greek mythology, the Rainbow Goddess is also messenger of the Gods, her name is 'Anuenue'. According to legend, this 'Rainbow Maiden' is so beautiful that a rainbow follows her everywhere she goes; For Ancient Hawaiian peoples the rainbow was so sacred and so special, that they carved it into petroglyphs on the big island's lava fields, and in the sacred Lao Valley of Maui. The depiction of a 'Man' and a 'Rainbow' in a petroglyph is interpreted as being the keeper of the land and its people; when a 'Woman' and an 'Arch' or a 'Rainbow' is present, it signifies she is wise, honored and respected.

Some Hawaiian natives say that each color of the rainbow is an aspect of a Goddess—the rainbow is the bridge that connects us to the 'Source'—and that meditating on a particular color will bring forth the manifestation of those intentions and elements representative of that shade.

This seems to make sense – there's that word "rain" in "rainbow" after all, and with good reason. For a rainbow to be formed, there need to be water droplets in the air. Then, light has to shine through those droplets at just the right angle. If this happens – voilà! A rainbow!

Krystaline Al-Shalaldeh

The Inka (Spanish transliterated 'Inca') indigenous people, whom had an empire that expanded to modern day parts of Argentina, Bolivia, Chile, Colombia, Ecuador, and Peru, contrary to popular belief were a conglomeration of several cultures, tribes, and languages. Inka was the name of the 'Ruling Class' and not the subjects of the empire. In this kingdom, the head ruler venerated the rainbow. This sacred symbol (banner) consisted of a 'Rainbow' with two parallel snakes on each side of the rainbow's end, and a tassle (symbolizing a type of crown) dangling down the middle of the rainbow's arch. This came to be known as Tawantinsuyu (Tawantin= Quartet/Group of Four – Suyu= Region), meaning the symbol for the 'Four Regions' (which is how the empire was broken up).

Similarly, the 'Whiphala' (co-official flag of Bolivia) is a square flag or emblem used to represent a variety of indigenous people's from the Andean regions, including some of the same people's as the Tawantinsuyu emblem. The suyu whiphalas are a 7-by-7 square patchwork, in seven colors arranged diagonally. The specific color pattern, or design, is determined by the 'Suyu' represented by the maker. Origins of both 'Tawantinsuyu' and 'Whiphala' can be traced back to symbols and mural designs found in several Andean civilizations with thousands of years of history.

There is also, in the same region, a seven striped 'Rainbow' flag in use today in Cusco, Peru, to represent Tawantinsuyu, or 'Inka Territory', and their struggle for indigenous rights/pride and cultural preservation, that can be traced back to the 1920s, and it is very much displayed with pride around the city, flying high above government buildings and in the main square. Different than the 'Gay Pride' rainbow flag, this flag carries 7 colors of the rainbow, instead of 6 like the former.

Interestingly, there are ruins called 'Huaca del Arco-Iris' (Temple of the Rainbow), in Trujillo Peru, and it depicts stone carvings and bass reliefs of designs similar to the Tawantinsuyu, however instead or parallel snakes, there are parallel 'Dragons' depicted. This symbol is repeated along most of the walls of this temple, and is an amazing and largest veneration (in the form of a pyramidal temple) to the rainbow. This ceremonial center was constructed of adobe and clay (with anti-seismic qualities), said to be dated about 1,100 years old by some.

Qaws-Quzah (pronounced Kaos Kuzajj) is one way to say rainbow in Arabic. In pre-Islamic times--before the Prophet Mohammed PBUH--the ancient people of Muzda'lifah (an area near Mecca in Saudi Arabia—associated with the Hajj Pilgrimage) believed in a deity, or supernatural being, by the name of Quzah. This being was believed to be a giant 'Divine Archer' who lived in the clouds and fired hail stones at demons. The rainbow was considered to be a 'bridge' to heaven. Their beliefs called Din Abā'i-ka, which means 'Faith of the Elders', is believed to be originated further back among the cousins of the Arabs, the Edomite Tribes of southwestern Jordan, who's main deity was 'Qaus'--which is also the Arabic word for bow or arch.

In Christianity, the rainbow is a significant sign, given directly from God—according to Christian texts—as a promise (covenant) to Noah. It is also considered to be, on a more broad basis, to be God's promise to mankind to preserve his creation, and the seven colors are the seven laws.

In European history, Germany in particular, Thomas Müntzer (1489-1525): 'Social Revolutionary' of the common people (peasants and plebeians) led the armed militia into the 'Peasant's War', against the feudal system of the time. Carried into battle, was a white banner (flag) depicting a rainbow, with the words written upon it "The Word of God will endure forever", symbolizing a new time of hope and change. A statue of Müntzer in Stolberg Germany shows him holding a flag with a rainbow on it.

"The Mandala—Tibetan sand painting—is an ancient art form of Tibetan Buddhism. The word 'Mandala' has its origin in Sanskrit, meaning 'cosmogram' or 'world in harmony', and is essentially a drawing in color-dyed sand particles. In Tibetan, this art is called dul-tson-kyil-khor which means "mandala of colored powders."
This multi-colored 'rainbow' sand painting is an ancient Tibetan art form, thought to have originated in India and then transplanted in the middle ages to Tibet. Although we say 'sand painting' in reality the mandala is a much more intricate 'sculpture' (three-dimensional work of art—or prayer) and requires many years of careful meditation, dedication, concentration, and contemplation on behalf of the meditator (artist/creator). Each detail is important,

Rainbow of Life! – NEW Book Preview

and based on very specific instructions and sacred meaning: Imbued into each action, is declaring specific intentions aimed at spreading compassion, realizing the illusionary banalities of reality, and subtle consciousness healing. There are great numbers of different mandalas, each with their own and unique lessons to teach, learn, observe, meditate upon, and blessings to impart.

Thomas Paine—American Revolutionary War Writer—suggested that a rainbow flag be used as a maritime flag for neutral ships during times of war.

In Sri Lanka, in 1885 a flag to represent Buddhism worldwide, and all its aspects, was designed of six vertical color segments. The first five colors are: Blue, yellow, red, white, orange, and the sixth is a combination of all other five colors.

Peace Movements all over the world have also used the rainbow flag emblem. James William van Kirk, from Ohio, USA, designed the first 'World Peace: Flag of Earth' using rainbow stripes, stars, and an interconnected globe attached by strings. In 1913 and again in 1929 he toured the world to introduce the flag. Universal Peace Congress adopted Kirk's flag, and it was subsequently adopted by American Peace Society and other groups.

In Basel, Switzerland 1921, a Congress of World Co-op Leaders met to asses and identify the common goals of the International Cooperative Movement and ideals to unite co-ops around the world. A French professor Charles Gide, proposed the seven color rainbow flag to show 'Unity in Diversity' and 'Power in Light', 'Enlightenment' and 'Progress' as concepts.

Meher Baba, Spiritual Master from India (of Irani decent), designed a rainbow flag in 1924. Baba explained "...the colors in the flag signify man's rise from the grossest of impressions of lust and anger—symbolized by red—to the spirituality and oneness with God—symbolized by sky blue."

In Italy there was a peace march in 1961, where the 'Peace' rainbow flag was used for the first time in more modern history. The flag holds seven colors of the rainbow horizontally, and the word 'PACE' (Italian for PEACE) written in white letters, centered in the middle. A previous version included a dove by Pablo Picasso. Greece also adopted this peace flag with Greek word for PEACE, as in the Italian version. This flag has since been adopted by the International Peace Movement and the word for 'PEACE' in different languages has been added in white to these as well.

In that same year (1961), there was a Jewish movement called 'Bene Ohr' meaning 'Children of Light', led by a Rabbi Zalman (Schachter-Shalomi). The story goes—as told by the rabbi himself—that one day he was meditating on the question 'How did God create the world?' He wrapped himself in a robe of light and it began to shine, says the rabbi. This was considered a beautiful inspiration and a vision was born to create a woven Jewish Prayer Shawl (Tallit), in vibrant rainbow colors. It was radical, but it was

Rainbow of Life! – NEW Book Preview

beautiful. Some older and more traditional members of the community labeled the idea a 'Purin Tallit' (Clown Tallit). Far from the misjudged assumptions, each color, width and arrangement of the black and white bands is based on the seven lower sephirot of the Kabbalistic Tree of Life. The colors represent aspects of God, while the black stripes and white spaces represent aspects of the creation and of protection.

And of course, we could not leave out the now famous LGBT (Gay Pride) Flag, which has unique and mixed origins on its own. In 1978 San Francisco, California artist Gilbert Baker originally created a flag with eight colors to symbolize diversity in the gay community. It was debuted in the 1978 Pride Parade in San Francisco as originally designed (with the 8 colors), however quickly it became apparent that there would be manufacturing issues, when instead of Indigo the fabric was replaced to the color Blue, because of availability, and in variations some carry purple instead of Violet. In 1979 a modified version of the flag would be paraded, and mass produced, however these new flags would be missing 2 colors: Pink and Turquoise, perhaps also for production reasons.

www.ingramcontent.com/pod-product-compliance
Lightning Source LLC
Chambersburg PA
CBHW041616220426
43671CB00001B/6